Turkish Cookery

Gülseren Ramazanoğlu

DAMKO

First published in June 1989   Sixth Edition, 1997
by Ramazanoğlu Publications
Edited by Gülseren Ramazanoğlu
Typeset by Mas Matbaacılık A.Ş.
Photography by Suat Eman Art direction by Joelle Danon
Color seperations by MAS Matbaacılık A.Ş.
Printed by MAS Matbaacılık A.Ş.

Published by DAMKO A.Ş.
Pehlivan Yanı Sok. Mineler Apt., A Blok, No. 11, Mecidiyeköy, Istanbul, Turkey
Tel.: (90-212) 213 25 55 - 213 25 56 - 213 25 57, Fax.: (90-212) 273 17 92

Distributed by Be-Ra Promosyon
Mail Order: Zeytinoğlu Cad., Bahar Sitesi, Mimoza 1, Daire 1, Akatlar, Istanbul, Turkey
Tel.: (90-212) 269 44 26 - 278 76 86, Fax.: (90-212) 278 68 96

COVER PHOTOGRAPHS, Front: White Kidney Bean and Meat Stew (see
page 65), a Turkish national dish. Back: Oriental Rice (left) (see page 86) and
Pilaf with Tomatoes (right) (see page 87).

Recipe contributions by:
Ahmet A. Ramazanoğlu *(fish soup)*; Berter Üner *(grilled meatballs, lady's thigh
meatballs, meat kebab, mussels hilati, oriental rice, semolina halva)*; Çolpan Kolsal
(semolina cake); Fatma İçkin *(yoghurt and mint soup)*; Gelik Restaurant *(rice with
mussels)*; Oktay Üner *(pumpkin dessert)*; Oya Yardımcı *(ravioli alla turca, savory pie)*;
Selahattin Çiçek *(Turkish bread)*; Verda Sorgun *(cream-stuffed apricots, fried carrots, fried
zucchinis)*.

Dishes prepared for photography by:
BEYTİ *(grilled meatballs, meat kebab, lamb chops)*; BORSA RESTAURANT *(assorted
stuffed vegetables - in olive oil, celery roots in olive oil, chicken with eggplant purée, semolina
halva, tomato and onion salad, white kidney bean and meat stew)*; GELIK RESTAURANT
(fish soup, grey mullet in olive oil, mackerel papilotte, poached sea bass); HILTON
INTERNATIONAL ISTANBUL *(almond pudding, beans pilaki, boiled lamb, chicken
casserole, circassian chicken, eggplant salad, eggplant with minced meal, eggs with minced
meat, eggs with shinach, fried meat fingers, green beans in olive oil, gurnard with
mayonnaise, lady's thigh meatballs, meat stew and eggplant purée, mussels pilaki, oriental
rice, poached eggs with yoghurt, red lentil soup, pilaf with tomato, savory rolls, schambled
eggs with tomato and pepperones, shepherd's salad, assorted stuffed vegetables, tomato and
rice soup, yoghurt and cucumber salad, white rice)*; GÜLEN GÜLER-Joelle Danon's cook
(lamb casserole, lamb with lettuce, artichoke in olive oil); KEMAL ORHAN - Şadiye
Turhan's cook - *(eggplants in olive oil, sardines in vine leaves, spinach with minced meat,
ravioli alla turca)*.

Crockeries, cutleries, glassware, tablecloths, copper dishes and accessories made
available for photography by: Hilton International Istanbul, Maria Gürmen, Olcay
Akkent, Seta Hidiş, Neslihan Savaş, Eleni Hristothoulo, Sarika Bornstein, Mary,
Eda and Joelle Danon, Stella Alguadiş.

Printed in Turkey

ISBN 975-7489-00-X

ACKNOWLEDGMENTS

I owe a debt of gratitude to my mother, husband and son for their contributions to finalize my recipes; to my best friend and colleague Berter Üner without whose meticulous and devoted collaboration I would not have realized this book; to my friend Şadiye Turhan and her chef Kemal Orhan; to the Hilton International Istanbul, Turkey's Premier Hotel and its chef Anno de Vries; to Borsa Lokantası, one of the oldest restaurants in Istanbul, and its chef I. Hakkı Günay; to Beyti, Istanbul's foremost meat restaurant, and its chef Mutallik Incekara; to Gelik, one of Istanbul's leading fish restaurants, and its chef Tamer Gündüz for taking all the trouble to prepare most of the dishes described in this book for us to photograph. Without their cooperations, I would have had to cook, all by myself, all the dishes rather than 45 of them.
I also owe much gratitude to the pleasant teamwork of the photographer Suat Eman and his assistant Hakan Süer and the graphic designer Joelle Danon who was also the art director for photography, to Betül Korzay for her excellent typesetting and to Hasan Yurtsever for running all the errands.

CONTENTS

HINTS
ABOUT TURKISH COOKING

Turkish cuisine is supposed to be one of the three great cuisines in the world, the others being Chinese and French.

Both Chinese and French cuisines originated in their native countries, while Turkish cuisine traveled from continent to continent and reached Anatolia, the crossroads of many civilizations. During its long travels over the centuries, Turkish cuisine interchanged culinary habits and recipes with other civilizations that it encountered. Therefore, it is rich in variety, tasty to different palates, and very healthy as it is supposed to be the most balanced cuisine.

All these characteristics rightly put Turkish cuisine on the pedestal it deserves.

SOUPS light or substantial, have a special place in the Turkish cuisine.

MEZE or Turkish hors d'oeuvre, an endless variety of small dishes, cold and hot, accompanies rakı, the Turkish national drink, distilled from grapes and flavored with aniseed. Rakı is supposed to be sipped slowly to an accompaniment of delicious food eaten slowly, to prevent a hang-over the following morning. Rakı sofrası or the 'rakı table', is the place to relax and enjoy life with friends or business partners.

The most popular "meze" varieties are melon, tomato, cucumber, Turkish white cheese, dolma in olive oil, eggplant salad, sigara börek (cheese rolls), fried eggplant, Circassian chicken (chicken with walnut sauce), bean plaki, fresh onions, mussels, fava (mashed broad bean salad), blanched almonds, çiroz (dried mackerel), lakerda (raw fish treated with salt), leblebi (roasted chick peas), black and green olives, radish, lettuce, "pastırma" (salted and spicy Turkish bacon), and "sucuk" (spicy Turkish salami.)

SALADS fresh or cooked are an important part of the Turkish meals. The most popular salad ingredients are lettuce, cucumber, onion, spring onion, tomato, bell pepper, pepperone, garlic, dill, parsley, mint and a series of raw or cooked vegetables. The national salad dressing is the mixture of olive oil, lemon juice and/or vinegar. Turks eat their salad together with their main course.

EGG DISHES in Turkish cuisine are served as quick meals rather than a breakfast treat.

MEAT is cooked in infinite varieties: baked, broiled, grilled, stewed, fried, kebabs, köftes (minced meat, bread crumbs, herbs and spices mixtures), cubed or minced meat stewed with vegetables or legumes, dolmas (a variety of vegetables stuffed with minced meat, rice, herbs and chopped onion mixtures.)

Lamb is supposed to be the national meat, and it tastes better in Turkey than anywhere else in the world because of the fragrance of the variety of herbs the lamb eats.

Most of the meat dishes, especially broiled ones and stews can be reheated.

POULTRY dishes do not abund in the Turkish cuisine and yet they are very unusual and tasty dishes.

FISH has a very special place in the Turkish cuisine. Turkey boasts of having a great variety of fish. Fish is prepared grilled, in papillote, fried, baked, broiled, steamed, dried, with mayonnaise, smoked and under treatment of salt.

Indigenous Turkish fish are lüfer (similar to blue fish), istavrit (like horse mackerel), çinekop (a kind of blue fish), çipura (similar to guilt head bream), hamsi (like anchovies) and izmarit (difficult to find a similar fish.) Travelers to Turkey should try any of the above fish.

VEGETABLES grow in abundance in Turkey. They are either cooked with meat and served hot or cooked in olive oil and served cold. Some of the vegetables are fried and served as an entrée. Many vegetables, mainly eggplant, are cooked in a great variety. Vegetable dishes are cooked with little amount of water to retain their food value and taste and they can be reheated.

RICE is used extensively in the Turkish cuisine, again in a great variety of ways and served as a side dish with meat and poultry, or as a second course after a light main meal.

BÖREK, rival to pilaf, occupies an important place in the Turkish culinary tradition. Böreks are made of yufka (readymade Turkish pastry dough or phyllo pastry) or made of dough rolled out in thin layers and filled with cheese, meat or spinach. Böreks are served as meze or as a second course.

TURKISH DESSERTS can be classified under four categories: pastry type (generally rich and sweet), puddings, cooked fruit desserts and fresh fruits. Fruit is abundant and varied in Turkey and tastes great. Traditionally most meals are concluded with fresh fruit.

COFFEE AND TEA are prepared in a special way. Coffee has an important place in Turkish hospitality. The English word coffee is derived from the Turkish word kahve. Although the coffee bean is a native of Ethiopia it was brought to Europe in the 16th century from Istanbul.

Mid-afternoon teas accompanied by cakes and cookies have an almost ritual quality in Turkish homes. As a matter of fact, food has always fulfilled a significant social function in Turkish society.

AYRAN (yoghurt drink) is as national as the cola drinks in the western world. Herbal teas are quite common as digestives or as a cure for upset stomachs.

TURKISH WINE in secular republican Turkey, graces many tables. One can find a great variety of table wines, almost in every city, as well as a great variety of cheeses.

The birthplace of wine was Asia minor, today's Turkey. The first vineyards in the world, dating back to 4000 BC, were traced by archaeologists in North Eastern Turkey. The objects found concerning grapes and wine from the Hittites (2000 BC) in Central Anatolia, prove that viniculture and wine-making were quite advanced. Moreover, the Hittite language contained the word "vino" meaning wine.

The knowledge and experience acquired during centuries of viniculture, combined with the soil and climatic conditions prevailing in Turkey, and the high quality of grapes grown here, have created the excellent Turkish wines. Cheers - in Turkish "Şerefe" (to your honor.)

Turks cook with feeling, devotion and imagination. Appreciation for good food is an incentive for the cook to prepare even better dishes. Turks mostly conclude a meal by saying "Elinize sağlık" to whoever cooked the meal. If translated literally it means "may God give health to your hands" in response to this, the cook says "afiyet olsun" (Bon appetit.)

Bon appetit to you for all the recipes you may venture to try from this book.

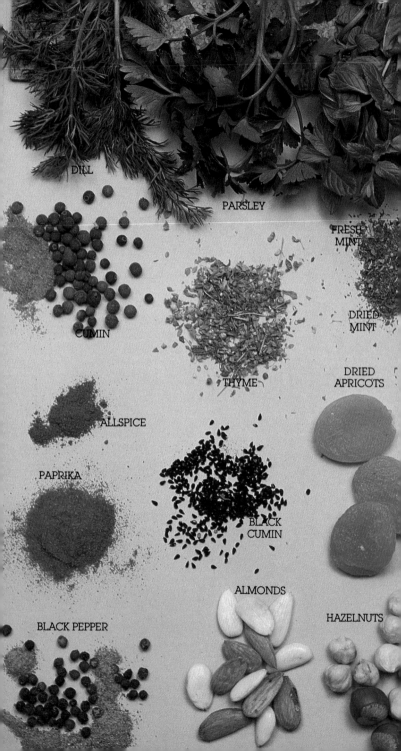

DILL

PARSLEY

FRESH MINT

CUMIN

THYME

DRIED MINT

ALLSPICE

DRIED APRICOTS

PAPRIKA

BLACK CUMIN

ALMONDS

BLACK PEPPER

HAZELNUTS

CINNAMON

CLOVES

BAY
LEAVES

CURRANTS

SULTANAS

COCONUTS

FIGS

PINE
NUTS

CHESTNUTS

PISTACHIO
NUTS

WALNUTS

LENTIL AND MINT SOUP
Ezo Gelin Çorbası

*1 cup (190 gr) red
lentils, soaked
overnight and
drained*

*8 cups (2 liters) beef
stock, chicken broth
or water*

1 onion, grated

*¼ cup (50 gr) rice or
bulgur (pounded
wheat)*

*2 tablespoons tomato
paste diluted in ¼
cup cold water*

¼ cup (50 gr) butter

salt to taste

1 teaspoon paprika

*1 tablespoon dried
mint*

Place lentils, stock, onion, rice, tomato
paste, butter and salt into a non-stick
saucepan. Cook while stirring
occasionally on very low heat until
lentils and rice are very tender and
the soup has a creamy consistency.

Add paprika and mint and let soup
simmer for 5 minutes.

12 servings.

CHICKEN SOUP WITH VERMICELLI
Şehriyeli Tavuk Çorbası

*4 cups (1 liter) chicken
  broth*
1 tablespoon butter
salt to taste
pepper (optional)
*½ cup (75 gr) broken
  vermicelli*
SAUCE
juice of 1 lemon
1 egg yolk

Place chicken broth, butter, salt and pepper into a saucepan. When it starts boiling, add vermicelli, stir to separate the strands and let it simmer for 5-10 minutes until vermicelli is cooked.

To prepare the egg and lemon sauce, beat the egg yolk until frothy. Add lemon juice beating constantly. Mix in to the mixture 1 cup of the hot broth continuing to beat. Then gradually pour it into the soup stirring constantly. Bring to a boil.
Serve immediately.
4 servings.

YOGHURT AND MINT SOUP
Yayla Çorbası

6 cups (1½ liters) beef
  stock or chicken
  broth
⅓ cup (70 gr) rice
3 tablespoons butter
2 cups (500 gr)
  yoghurt
1 heaped tablespoon
  flour
2 egg yolks
salt to taste
DRESSING
¼ cup (50 gr) butter
¼ cup (15 gr) dried·
  mint

Bring beef stock or chicken broth to a
boil, and add rice and butter. Simmer
over low heat until rice is well cooked.

Mix yoghurt, flour and egg yolks
together in a bowl and add salt. Stir
the mixture into the boiling beef
broth and rice, and let it simmer for
15 minutes until the soup has a
creamy consistency.

Melt butter in a small saucepan, then
add dried mint and stir for 1 minute.
Garnish with mint dressing.
6 servings.

RED LENTIL SOUP
Süzme Mercimek Çorbası

1 cup (190 gr) red
  lentils, soaked
  overnight and
  drained
6 cups (1½ liters) water
  or chicken broth or
  beef stock
2 medium onions,
  grated
2 carrots, grated
1 teaspoon paprika
salt to taste
2 tablespoons butter
2 cups (500 ml)
  tomato juice or 2
  tablespoons tomato
  paste diluted in ¼
  cup cold water
DRESSING
1 tablespoon butter
½ tablespoon paprika

Place lentils, water or broth, onions,
carrots, paprika and salt into a
saucepan. Cook until lentils are
tender. Remove from heat and press
through a sieve (the residue is to be
thrown away) or blend in a food
processor or in a blender. Add butter
and tomato paste and bring to a boil.

Melt 1 tablespoon butter in a pan,
add ½ tablespoon paprika, stir and
trickle over the soup.

The consistency of the soup should
be creamy. Butter and paprika
dressing may be replaced by croûtons.
6 servings.

TOMATO AND RICE SOUP
Domatesli Pirinç Çorbası

⅓ cup (70 gr) rice
   (short grain)
3 large ripe tomatoes
6 cups (1½ liters) beef
   stock or water
1 tablespoon butter
salt and pepper to taste
½ cup (30 gr) parsley,
   chopped

Wash rice and put into a saucepan
with grated tomatoes, beef stock,
butter, salt and pepper. Bring to a boil
without the lid on. Cover and simmer
until rice is very tender.

Garnish with finely chopped parsley.
6 servings.

15

WEDDING SOUP
Düğün Çorbası

2 lbs (900 gr) mutton
  bones with some
  meat on it or beef
  neck
1 medium onion, cut
  into quarters
1 medium carrot,
  scraped
12 cups (3 liters)
  water
salt to taste
½ cup (100 gr) butter
⅓ cup (35 gr) flour
2 egg yolks
juice of 1 lemon
DRESSING
1 tablespoon paprika
1 tablespoon butter

Place bones, onion and carrot into a saucepan. Add water and salt and bring to a boil. Remove the foam off the top with a skimmer. Cover the saucepan and let it simmer for 2 hours until the meat is tender. Remove from heat. Strain the broth into another saucepan, shred the meat from the bones and add to the broth. Put butter into a big saucepan over low heat. When it melts, add flour and stir constantly with a wooden spoon until blended. Pour the meat stock into this mixture gradually while stirring constantly. Bring to a boil. Then remove from heat.

Beat the egg yolks and lemon juice together in a clean bowl and stir in 2 cups of steaming hot soup. Then pour this mixture into the hot soup and stir once. The consistency should be creamy. If necessary hot water can be added to thin the soup.

Sauté paprika with 1 tablespoon butter in a pan. Pour soup into a serving bowl or individual soup dishes. Trickle the paprika dressing over the top and serve with croûtons.
8 servings.

FISH SOUP
Balık Çorbası

2 lbs (900 gr) deep sea
  fish (fish with white
  flesh)
1 teaspoon salt
1 cup (60 gr) parsley,
  chopped
½ onion
1 clove garlic
3 cups (750 ml) water
¼ cup (50 ml) olive oil
¼ cup (25 gr) flour
salt and pepper to taste
1 cup (60 gr) parsley,
  chopped
SAUCE
½ cup (125 ml) lemon
  juice
2 egg yolks

Gut and wash the fish. Put the fish into a big saucepan, and add salt and 1 cup finely chopped parsley, onion and garlic. Add water and let it simmer over medium heat until the fish begins to flake itself. Strain the stock into another saucepan. Remove the skin and bones from the cooked fish. Break the fish into small pieces. Bring the stock to a boil, then add the flaked fish and simmer for 10 minutes to make a soup.

Pour olive oil into a small saucepan, add flour and stir it constantly over low heat. Pour 1 cup of fish soup over and let it simmer for 10 minutes still stirring. Add this mixture to the soup, then add salt and pepper to taste. Remove from heat.

Mix lemon juice and egg yolks together in a small bowl and stir this mixture into the soup before serving. Garnish with 1 cup chopped parsley.

NOTE
4 lbs (1800 gr) fish scraps (the head, tail and bones of fish) with white flesh may be used instead of a whole fish.

6 servings.

HORS D'OEUVRES
MEZE
SAVORY ROLLS

MUSSELS PİLAKİ
Midye Pilakisi

1 large onion, chopped
6 tablespoons salad or
  olive oil
2 carrots, diced
80-100 mussels,
  cleaned and washed
2 medium potatoes,
  diced
1 large tomato,
  skinned and chopped
1 cup (250 ml) water
2-3 cloves garlic, diced
1 tablespoon sugar
salt and pepper to taste
$\frac{1}{2}$ cup (30 ml) parsley,
  chopped

Sauté onion in oil over medium heat for 5 minutes stirring constantly, add carrots and sauté for another 5 minutes. Add the well-drained mussels, potatoes, tomato, water, garlic, sugar, salt and pepper. Cook over medium heat for half an hour and then on very low heat for 15-20 minutes until the water is absorbed by the vegetables.

Add chopped parsley and allow to cool.

8 servings.

BEANS PİLAKİ
Fasulye Pilaki

1$\frac{1}{2}$ cups (300 gr) white
  kidney beans or
  pinto beans
4 cups (1 liter) water
$\frac{1}{2}$ cup (100 ml) olive
  oil or salad oil
2 onions, chopped
2 carrots, diced
2 potatoes, diced
2 tablespoons tomato
  paste, diluted in $\frac{1}{4}$
  cup cold water
4 cloves garlic,
  chopped
1 tablespoon sugar
salt to taste
3 cups (750 ml) hot
  water
GARNISH
1 cup (60 gr) parsley,
  chopped
8 lemon wedges
juice of 2 lemons

Soak the beans overnight in plenty of salted water, drain and wash.

Boil the beans in 4 cups of water until they are almost tender, drain. Set aside.

Place oil and chopped onions in a saucepan and sauté for 5 minutes stirring constantly, add carrots and continue stirring for another 5 minutes. Then add beans, potatoes, tomato paste, garlic, sugar, salt and water. Cook over medium heat for 20 minutes, then lower the heat and cook for another 30 minutes until beans are tender and the dish has enough gravy.

Transfer to a serving platter. Garnish with chopped parsley and lemon wedges. Serve cold as an appetizer with lemon juice.

8 servings.

EGGPLANT SALAD
Patlıcan Salatası

3 large eggplants,
  unpeeled
2 tablespoons lemon
  juice
⅓ cup (70 ml) olive oil
  or salad oil
salt to taste
2 cloves garlic, crushed
2 cups (500 gr)
  yoghurt
GARNISH
1 tomato cut into 8
  wedges
1 green bell pepper,
  seeded and sliced
½ cup (30 gr) parsley,
  chopped
6 black olives

Pierce the eggplants with a fork. Place them in a pan over an open flame or on a high gas flame or on charcoal and cook them for half an hour, turning them often until the skin blisters on all sides and the eggplant becomes soft. Cool. Cut eggplant lengthways into two.

Scoop out the pulp, squeeze out all the moisture and mash with a fork on a wooden board. Place the eggplant pulp into a bowl and add lemon juice, olive oil, salt, garlic and yoghurt. Mash until it becomes like purée.

Place on a serving bowl and garnish with tomato, bell pepper, parsley and black olives. Chill for ½ hour before serving.
6 servings.

SAVORY ROLLS
Sigara Böreği

CHEESE FILLING

2 cups (400 gr)
  Turkish white cheese,
  crumbled or feta or
  cottage cheese
2 tablespoons Turkish
  kaşar or kashkaval
  or parmesan cheese,
  grated
1 egg
salt (if wanted)
1 cup (60 gr) parsley,
  chopped
1 cup (60 gr) dill,
  chopped

MEAT FILLING

½ lb (225 gr) minced
  beef
1 onion, grated
1 tablespoon butter
1 small tomato, grated
¼ cup (30 gr) parsley,
  chopped
salt and pepper to taste

VARIETY FILLINGS

Spinach purée or
sliced sausages cooked
in butter and tomato
juice can also be used
as fillings.

PASTRY

3 phyllo sheets or 2
  yufka sheets
  (unleavened pastry)
⅓ cup (70 gr) melted
  butter (for baking)
½ cups (125 ml) cold
  water (for sealing)
1 egg yolk (for
  brushing tops)
1½ cups (300 ml)
  salad oil (for frying)

CHEESE FILLING

Put cheeses, egg, salt, parsley and dill in a bowl, mix with a fork. Set aside.

MEAT FILLING

Sauté meat in frying pan with onion and butter for 10 minutes. Add tomato, parsley, salt and pepper and cook for another 10 minutes. Set aside.

Pile pastries or yufkas on top of each other and cut with a sharp knife.
Phyllo pastry: Cut lengthways into 6 strips. Cut each strip into 2, obtaining 12 strips from one sheet.
Circular shaped Turkish yufka: Cut into 4. Divide each quarter into 4. 16 triangles are obtained from one sheet. If smaller rolls are preferred for cocktails, one circular sheet can yield up to 24 triangles.

FOR BAKING

Brush pastry strips generously with melted butter. Place one teaspoon of cheese or meat or spinach or sausage filling in one end. In the case of triangles, place filling across the base of each triangle. Tuck in ½ inch (1 cm) of pastry on both sides over the filling, roll up. Damp the end with water for sealing. Brush the top of the rolls with egg yolk. Lightly grease the baking pan. Bake in moderate oven until they are crisp and golden brown. Serve hot.

FOR FRYING

Do not butter pastry strips. Fill the rolls as described for baking. Put oil in a big pan and heat. Place rolls in hot oil and fry them until golden brown. They can also be deep fried.

8 servings.

CIRCASSIAN CHICKEN
Çerkez Tavuk

3¼ lbs (1575 gr)
  stewing chicken
1 large onion,
  quartered
salt and pepper to taste
8 cups (2 liters) water
WALNUT SAUCE
3¼ cups (350 gr)
  walnuts, shelled and
  chopped
4 slices day-old white
  bread, torn into
  small pieces
salt to taste
1 tablespoon minced
  onion
1 clove garlic, crushed
  (optional)
1 teaspoon paprika
1 cup (250 ml) chicken
  broth
DRESSING
1 tablespoon salad oil
1 teaspoon paprika

Wash and place chicken, onion, salt and pepper into a saucepan with water. Bring to a boil. Cook over medium heat until chicken is tender. Remove chicken from saucepan and cool. Remove skin and bones and cut it into small strips. Set aside, reserve the stock.

Grind the walnuts through a meat grinder. Remove the crust from the bread, soak in water and squeeze dry. Mix with ground walnuts in a bowl. Add salt, minced onion, garlic and paprika. Blender may also be used. Add chicken broth gradually until creamy consistency is obtained.

Place chicken on a serving platter, toss gently with half of walnut sauce. Spread the rest of sauce on top.

Place oil in a saucepan over low heat, add paprika and heat for 1 minute and trickle paprika dressing over the walnut sauce.

Serve at room temperature.

8 servings.

SALADS

TOMATO AND ONION SALAD
CARROT AND YOGHURT SALAD
SPINACH ROOT SALAD

SHEPHERD's SALAD
Çoban Salatası

2 large tomatoes, diced
2 cucumbers, diced
3 pepperones, chopped
6 radishes, thinly sliced
1 onion, sliced into
* rings*
½ cup (30 gr) parsley,
* chopped*
LEMON DRESSING
6 tablespoons lemon
* juice*
¼ cup (50 ml) olive oil
salt and pepper to taste

Combine all ingredients in a bowl. Mix all ingredients together and gently toss salad with the lemon dressing just before servings.
4 servings.

SPINACH ROOTS SALAD
Ispanak Kökü Salatası

4 lbs (1800 gr)
  spinach
1 cup (250 ml) boiling
  water
salt and pepper to taste
DRESSING
½ cup (100 ml) olive
  oil or salad oil
6 tablespoons lemon
  juice

Use only the roots of the spinach. Cut off the stems. Wash well and place in a saucepan with 1 cup of boiling water. Cook uncovered for about 10 minutes. Drain and season with salt and pepper.

Place boiled spinach roots in a salad bowl. Mix olive oil and lemon juice together. Pour over the roots and toss. **8 servings.**

TOMATO AND ONION SALAD
Soğanlı Domates Salatası

4 large ripe tomatoes
1 large onion
2 teaspoons salt
LEMON DRESSING
¼ cup (50 ml) olive
  oil or salad oil
5 tablespoons lemon
  juice
salt and pepper to taste
½ cup (30 gr) parsley,
  chopped
VINEGAR
DRESSING
¼ cup (50 ml) olive or
  salad oil
¼ cup (62.5 ml)
  vinegar
½ cup (30 gr) parsley,
  chopped
salt to taste

Wash, skin and seed tomatoes. Cut crosswise slices. Slice the onion finely. Sprinkle with salt, rub in, rinse and squeeze dry. Place tomatoes and onions into a salad bowl.

Mix olive oil, lemon juice, salt and pepper together. Pour this dressing over the tomatoes and onions, toss. Garnish with parsley.

VARIATION
Peeled and sliced cucumber can be added to the tomato and onion salad.

Onion salad can be made without tomatoes. Cut 2 large onions into very fine slices. Place in a bowl with salt. Knead. Wash with water several times, squeeze dry with hand. Spread on a salad platter. Serve with vinegar dressing.

Tomato salad can be made without onions and served with lemon dressing.
8 servings.

YOGHURT AND CUCUMBER
SALAD Cacık

1 clove garlic
3 large cucumbers
4 cups (1 kg) yoghurt
salt to taste
2 cloves garlic, crushed
2 tablespoons fresh
mint, chopped or
1 tablespoon dried
mint
6 tablespoons dill,
chopped
½ cup (125 ml) water
(optional)
4 tablespoons olive
or salad oil
GARNISH
12 mint leaves

Rub a salad bowl with 1 garlic clove. Peel and dice cucumbers. Place cucumbers into the garlic-rubbed bowl.

Beat yoghurt and salt together until creamy. Pour this over cucumbers. Add crushed garlic, mint and dill. Stir until the mixture has a thick consistency. Add water if necessary and beat well in.

Trickle olive oil on top and sprinkle mint leaves to garnish. Cover and chill in refrigerator. Serve cold with ice cubes in individual bowls as an hors d'oeuvre or as a salad or as a cold luncheon soup in summer.
6 servings.

CARROT SALAD WITH YOGHURT
Havuç Salatası

4 large carrots
3 cups (750 ml) water
DRESSING
1½ cups (375 gr)
yoghurt
4 cloves garlic, crushed
2 tablespoons lemon
juice
1 tablespoon olive oil
salt to taste
¼ cup (15 gr) chopped
parsley

Scrap and wash carrots. Half cook in boiling water in full. Drain and cool. Grate carrots into a salad bowl.

Mix yoghurt, garlic, lemon juice, olive oil and salt. Add this mixture to carrots, mix well. Garnish with chopped parsley.
6 servings.

EGG DISHES
SCRAMBLED EGGS
POACHED EGGS

SCRAMBLED EGGS WITH TOMATOES   Menemen

1 tablespoon butter 4 medium tomatoes, skinned and sliced 4 pepperones, chopped salt and pepper to taste 4 eggs ⅓ cup (20 gr) parsley (optional)	Melt butter in a pan, add tomatoes and pepperones, salt and pepper. Cover and cook until they are tender and ooze liquid. Beat the eggs in a bowl, gradually add into the tomato and pepperone mixture. Continue stirring. Add chopped parsley just before the eggs are set and stir once. **4 servings.**

POACHED EGGS WITH YOGHURT
Çılbır

2 cups (500 gr) yoghurt 1 teaspoon salt 4 large eggs 4 cups (1 liter) boiling water 1 tablespoon vinegar salt to taste DRESSING 1 tablespoon butter 1 teaspoon paprika	Beat yoghurt and 1 teaspoon salt with a fork until smooth. Put aside. Poach eggs in boiling water with vinegar until the whites are set. Transfer eggs to a serving dish with a perforated spoon. Sprinkle with salt. Pour yoghurt over the eggs. Melt butter in a small saucepan and add paprika. Trickle this dressing on top of the yoghurt. Serve immediately. **4 servings.**

EGGS WITH MINCED MEAT
Kıymalı Yumurta

1 tablespoon butter 1 large onion, grated ½ lb (225 gr) minced meat 1 tomato, diced ½ teaspoon salt 4 eggs salt and pepper to taste	Melt butter in a non-stick pan, add onion and fry until golden brown. Add minced meat, stir and fry until meat simmers, add tomato and ¼ teaspoon salt still stirring for another 2 minutes. Spread this mixture over the pan. Make spaces for 4 eggs. Break eggs one by one into each space, sprinkle with salt and pepper. Cover and cook on a very low heat until eggs are set. Serve immediately. **4 servings.**

EGGS WITH SPINACH
Ispanaklı Yumurta

1 lb (450 gr) spinach
2 tablespoons butter
1 large onion, grated
salt and pepper to taste
2 cups (500 ml) milk
*   or chicken broth*
4 eggs

Cut off roots of spinach, wash and drain the leaves. Chop them finely. Place into a pan, cook uncovered without additional water. Turn with fork frequently.

Cook for 8-10 minutes. Drain. Squeeze the remaining water out. Melt butter in a saucepan, sauté onions, add salt, pepper and spinach, stir with a wooden spoon, add milk or chicken broth, sauté until spinach absorbs all liquid and becomes puréed. Spread it over the pan. Make spaces for 4 eggs and break eggs one by one into each space. Cook covered over a very low heat until the eggs are set.

4 servings.

MEATS
AND POULTRY
GARDENER'S MEAT BALLS

MEAT STEW
Tas Kebap

2 medium onions,
  grated
2 tablespoons butter
2 lbs (900 gr) meat,
  cut into 1 inch (2.5
  cm) cubes (lamb,
  mutton or veal)
3 medium tomatoes,
  skinned, seeded and
  chopped, or 2
  tablespoons tomato
  paste, diluted in $\frac{1}{4}$
  cup cold water
salt and pepper to taste
$\frac{1}{2}$ teaspoon thyme
1 cup (250 ml) boiling
  water

Sauté onions in butter, stirring constantly for 5 minutes until they are lightly browned. Add meat and continue stirring for another 5 minutes. Cover and cook over low heat until the meat releases its moisture and reabsorbs it. Add tomatoes or tomato paste, salt, pepper, thyme and 1 cup of boiling water, and cook over medium heat for 1 hour. Lower heat and cook for another 20 minutes until the meat is tender and has a thick gravy.

A little hot water may be added at a time if necessary.

Serve hot as a main course with pilaf, or eggplant purée (see page 67)
6 servings.

BOILED LAMB
Kuzu Haşlama

2 lbs (900 gr) lamb in
large pieces on the
bone
2 whole onions
salt and pepper to taste
8 cups (2 liters) water
4 small potatoes,
peeled and quartered
4 carrots, scraped and
cubed
$\frac{1}{2}$ cup (30 gr) parsley,
chopped

Place meat in a saucepan, add onions, salt, pepper and water. Bring to a boil. Cover. Simmer for 1 hour, then add potatoes and carrots. Simmer until meat is tender and vegetables are cooked and there is plenty of liquid. Hot water can be added if necessary. Remove onions. Sprinkle with chopped parsley.

Serve in individual soup dishes as a main course.

6 servings.

LAMB CASSEROLE
Kuzu Güveç

½ lb (225 gr) green beans
3 large tomatoes
1 medium eggplant
¼ lb (112.5 gr) okra
2 medium zucchinis
3 green bell peppers
2 onions, chopped
2 cloves garlic, chopped
2 tablespoons butter
2 lbs (900 gr) lamb, cut into cubes of 1 inch (2.5 cm)
½ cup (125 ml) water
2 bay leaves
2 medium potatoes
salt and pepper to taste
1 tablespoon butter

Top, tail and string the beans. Skin tomatoes and cut into wedges. Cut off the stem of the eggplant, peel in strips and slice crosswise. Trim cone-shaped ends of the okra. Scrap and slice zucchinis. Seed and cut bell peppers into 8.

Sauté onions and garlic in butter, add meat, sauté for 15 minutes, add water and bay leaves. Cover. Simmer until the meat is tender. Transfer the meat mixture to an earthenware casserole.

Arrange potatoes in layer on top of the meat. Then place green beans, half of tomatoes, eggplants, okra, zucchinis, rest of tomatoes and bell peppers in layers.

Add salt and pepper and dot with butter. Cover and bake in moderate oven until vegetables are tender. Hot water can be added, if necessary.

Serve hot as a main course with pilaf and salad.

8 servings.

LAMB WITH LETTUCE
Kuzu Kapama

3 medium size lettuces
3 lbs (1350 gr) leg of lamb cut into 2 inch (5 cm) chunks
½ lemon (for rubbing the meat)
1 tablespoon butter
1 onion, sliced into rings
10 spring onions, thickly sliced

Separate lettuce leaves, wash and place them at the bottom of a large and heavy saucepan.

Rub meat with lemon. Place meat chunks over lettuce leaves. Add butter, onion, spring onions, sugar, salt, pepper and water. Cover. Cook over very low heat until meat is tender for about an hour. Add dill just before transferring to a serving platter. Serve hot as a main course with pilaf.

1 tablespoon sugar
salt and pepper to taste
½ cup (125 ml) water
1 cup (60 gr) dill,
  chopped

**EGG AND LEMON
SAUCE**

2 egg yolks
1 tablespoon flour
2 tablespoons lemon
  juice

VARIATION

Lettuce can be replaced by Swiss chard. This dish may be served with the egg and lemon sauce.

Blend egg yolks and flour together. Stir in lemon juice and 1 cup of meat stock from the saucepan. Beat in well. Return the mixture to the saucepan. Stir.

4 servings.

GRILLED LAMB CHOPS
Kuzu Pirzola

MARINADE
2 large onions, grated
1 teaspoon salt
3 tablespoons salad oil

12 loin lamb chops
2 tablespoons thyme
salt to taste

Sprinkle grated onions with salt, squeeze out the juice of the onions and mix this with oil. Brush lamb chops on both sides with this marinade, and leave to stand for 1 hour.

Grill chops, preferably over charcoal, on both sides. Sprinkle with thyme and salt.

Serve hot as a main course with pilaf or French fried potatoes.
4 servings.

MEAT KEBAB
Şiş Kebap

2 lbs (900 gr) lamb or
  beef cut into cubes
MARINADE
1 teaspoon salt
1 teaspoon pepper
1 tablespoon tomato
  paste
1 teaspoon mustard
1 teaspoon thyme
1 tablespoon yoghurt
1 onion, grated
1 tablespoon olive oil
TO THREAD ON
SKEWERS
4 tomatoes, seeded and
  quartered or 12
  cherry tomatoes
4 green bell peppers,
  seeded and cut into 2
  inch (5 cm) squares
12 pearl onions,
  peeled or 3 onions,
  quartered

Place meat in a bowl, add salt, pepper, tomato paste, mustard, thyme, yoghurt, onion and olive oil. Mix well, cover and refrigerate overnight to marinate.

Arrange meat on skewers alternately with tomatoes, peppers and pearl onions.

Broil over charcoal about 3-4 inches (7-10 cm) away from the fire for about 15-20 minutes turning constantly to get the meat evenly cooked.

Serve hot on the skewers as a main course with pilaf and salad.
6 servings.

FRIED MEAT FINGERS
Kuru Köfte

1 lb (450 gr) minced
   meat
1 large onion, grated
3 slices of day-old
   bread, crust
   removed, bread
   soaked in water and
   squeezed dry
salt and pepper to taste
2 eggs
$\frac{1}{2}$ cup (30 gr) parsley,
   chopped
$\frac{1}{4}$ cup (62.5 ml) water
$\frac{1}{2}$ cup (50 gr) flour ·
   (optional for coating)
salad oil, 1 inch (2.5
   cm) deep in the
   frying pan

Combine meat, onion, bread, salt, pepper, eggs, parsley and water in a bowl. Knead well until all ingredients blend. Wet palms and form finger shapes about 1 inch (2.5 cm) thick. To obtain a smooth crust, roll meat fingers in flour before frying. Heat salad oil in a frying pan over medium heat. Fry both sides of meat fingers until brown.

Serve hot with French fried potatoes and salad as a casual main course or serve cold as a light luncheon dish with salad.

A favorite dish for picnics.
5 servings.

LADY'S THIGH MEATBALLS
Kadınbudu Köfte

$\frac{1}{4}$ cup (50 gr) rice
2 cups water
2 small onions, grated
1 lb (450 gr) minced
  meat
$1\frac{1}{2}$ tablespoons butter
2 eggs
salt and pepper to taste
salad oil, 1 inch (2.5
  cm) deep in the
  frying pan

Boil rice in 2 cups of water until it is
tender. Drain and set aside.

Sauté onions and half of the meat
($\frac{1}{2}$ lb) in butter over medium heat for
5-10 minutes until meat releases its
moisture and reabsorbs it. Remove
from heat. Add remaining raw meat,
cooked rice, 1 egg, salt and pepper.
Knead well. Shape 2 tablespoons of
meat mixture into small ovals. Dip
them into the remaining 1 beaten egg.
Fry on both sides in hot oil until
golden brown.

Serve hot as a main course with
green vegetables, boiled potatoes and
salad.

5 servings.

GRILLED MEATBALLS
Cızbız Köfte

2 lbs (900 gr) minced mutton, lamb or veal
1 large onion, grated
4 slices of day-old white bread, crusts removed, bread soaked in water and squeezed dry
1 clove garlic, grated (optional)
1 tablespoon olive oil
½ teaspoon cumin
salt and pepper to taste
1 teaspoon baking soda

Place minced meat, onion, bread, garlic, olive oil, cumin, salt, pepper and baking soda in a bowl. Knead well together until all ingredients blend. Pick up the kneaded meat with two hands, lift it and throw it on the hard surface of the kitchen counter. Repeat this process ten times.

Wet palms with water and shape meat mixture into small ovals and flatten them. Set aside.

Brush grid with olive oil and grill the meatballs on both sides. Serve immediately with rice or French fried potatoes, grilled tomatoes and pepperones. Electric broiler or a non-stick pan can also be used.

10 servings

MEATBALLS WITH EGG AND LEMON SAUCE Terbiyeli Köfte

*1 lb (450 gr) minced
    beef
¼ cup (50 gr) rice
salt and pepper to taste
1 cup (60 gr) parsley,
    finely chopped
½ cup (50 gr) flour
5 cups (1 ¼ liters) water
1 whole onion
2 tablespoons butter
4 carrots, diced
4 potatoes, diced
    (optional)*

Place meat into a bowl, add rice, salt, pepper and parsley. Knead well together. Wet palms and form walnut-size meatballs. Place them into a bowl with flour and shake until meatballs are coated with the flour.

Bring water to a boil, add onion, butter, carrots and salt. Transfer meatballs gently into the boiling water. Add potatoes when meatballs are half-cooked. Simmer for about half an hour on lowest possible heat until meatballs are cooked. Remove from heat and discard the cooked onion.

continued on the next page

SAUCE
2 eggs
4 tablespoons lemon juice

Break the eggs into a bowl and beat with the lemon juice. Gradually add 4 tablespoons of broth from the meatballs and stir. Return this sauce to the meatballs. Stir once. The dish should have plenty of gravy.

Serve hot as a main course in individual soup bowls.

6 servings.

GARDENER'S MEATBALLS
Bahçıvan Köftesi

1 medium eggplant, peeled in strips and sliced
2 teaspoons salt
1½ lbs (675 gr) minced meat
1 large onion, grated
2½ slices of day-old white bread, crusts removed, bread soaked in water and squeezed dry
2 eggs
1 cup (60 gr) dill, chopped
salt and pepper to taste
2 large potatoes, cubed
1 cup (200 ml) salad oil
1 cup (100 gr) canned peas
2 large tomatoes, skinned and sliced
2 cups (500 ml) water
2 tablespoons butter

Sprinkle eggplant with 2 teaspoons salt and set aside for an hour. Wash off excess salt and drain.

Combine meat, onion, bread, eggs, dill, salt and pepper in a bowl. Knead for 5 minutes until all ingredients blend. Wet palms and form walnut-size meatballs, flatten them slightly. Set aside.

Sauté potatoes in salad oil until golden brown and set aside. Fry eggplants and then meatballs in the same pan until golden brown and transfer them to a heat-resistant dish preferably earthenware. Add peas, tomatoes and water. Sprinkle with salt and pepper. Dot with butter. Cook covered over medium heat for about 20 minutes, until meatballs and vegetables are tender.

Add sautéed potatoes. Bring to a boil once and remove from heat. A small amount of water can be added if necessary.

Serve hot as a main course with rice and salad.

8 servings.

CHICKEN AND VEGETABLE STEW
Sebzeli Tavuk Yahnisi

4 lbs (1800 gr)
chicken, cut into
serving portions
1 cup (200 ml) salad
oil
4 tomatoes, sliced
4 carrots, cubed
1 cup (100 gr) peas,
drained
2 small onions, grated
2 cloves garlic
2 cups (500 ml)
chicken broth
2 tablespoons butter
salt and pepper to taste
3 large potatoes, cubed

Sauté chicken on all sides in hot oil until golden brown. Transfer to a casserole. Add tomatoes, carrots, peas, onions and garlic. Pour chicken broth over, dot with butter, sprinkle with pepper and salt. Cover, stew and simmer over low heat. When vegetables are half cooked, add potatoes. Simmer until chicken is tender and vegetables are cooked.

Serve hot as a main dish with rice.
8 servings.

CHICKEN CASSEROLE
Piliç Güveç

2 lbs (900 gr)
  chicken, cut into
  serving portions
¼ cup (50 ml) salad
  oil
¼ lb (110 gr) fresh
  okra or dry okra,
  boiled and drained
½ lb (225 gr) eggplants
½ lb (225 gr) string
  beans
4 tomatoes
2 green bell peppers
2 onions, grated
salt and pepper to taste
2 cups (500 ml)
  chicken broth
2 teaspoons butter
12 pearl onions

Sauté chicken pieces in salad oil for 15 minutes. Set aside.

Peel cone-shaped ends of the okra. Peel eggplants in strips and slice thickly. Top, tail and string the beans and cut them into two pieces. Skin, seed and slice tomatoes. Cut bell peppers into strips. Wash onions and vegetables and place them into a big casserole (preferably earthenware) in layers except for pearl onions, tomatoes and bell peppers. Season with salt and pepper. Place chicken pieces, tomatoes and bell peppers on top of the vegetables. Pour chicken broth over. Dot with butter. Garnish with pearl onions and cover.

Pre-heat the oven to 350ºF (180ºC) and cook for about an hour, until chicken is tender and vegetables are cooked. Serve with rice from the casserole as a main course.
4 servings.

CHICKEN WITH EGGPLANT
PURÉE Beğendili Tavuk

*1 medium size chicken,
   cut into serving
   portions or 4 chicken
   breasts*
*salt and pepper for
   seasoning*
*½ cup (100 ml) salad
   oil*
*2 large tomatoes,
   grated*
*1 cup (250 ml) chicken
   broth*
1 tablespoon butter
salt and pepper to taste
SIDE DISH
*Eggplant purée
(see page 67)*

Wash and season chicken pieces with salt and pepper. Sauté chicken pieces in salad oil for 15 minutes on medium heat. Add tomatoes, chicken broth, butter, salt and pepper to taste.

Cook covered over low heat until chicken is tender and most of the tomato juice is absorbed.

Arrange chicken pieces around a serving platter. Fill the center with eggplant purée. Serve hot as a main dish.

VARIATION
Stewed chicken can be replaced by roast or grilled chicken.
4 servings.

FISH
SARDINES IN VINE LEAVES

POACHED SEA BASS
Levrek Buğulama

2 medium sea bass,
  sliced or 4 fillets
  from a large sea bass
¼ cup (50 gr) salad oil
1 small can
  mushrooms, sliced
3 pepperones, sliced
4 medium tomatoes,
  grated
salt and pepper to taste
1 lemon, sliced thin
2 bay leaves
1 cup (60 gr) parsley,
  chopped

Gut the fish, wash and drain. Set aside.

Heat salad oil, add mushrooms, green pepperones and stir for 5 minutes over medium heat. Add tomatoes, salt and pepper, stir for another 5 minutes.

Place sea bass in a heat-resistant serving dish, shallow and wide and pour tomato mixture over the fish. Top with lemon slices and bay leaves. Cover.

Cook over medium heat until fish is tender for approximately 15 minutes. Garnish with parsley.

Serve at room temperature as a main course with boiled potatoes and salad.
4 servings.

MACKEREL PAPILLOTE

Uskumru Kağıtta

4 big or 8 small
   mackerel
salt
1 tablespoon salad oil
4 pieces wax paper,
   10 x 10 inches
   (25 x 25 cm)
2 tomatoes, sliced
8 lemon slices
1 small can
   mushrooms, sliced
freshly ground pepper
   to taste
$\frac{1}{2}$ cup (30 gr) parsley,
   chopped
$\frac{1}{2}$ lb (225 gr) kaşar
   (see page 84) or
   parmesan grated
4 teaspoons water for
   sprinkling

Gut and wash each fish, drain and rub with salt.

Brush oil on each piece of wax paper. Place 1 big mackerel or 2 small ones on each of the pieces. Place tomato, lemon slices and mushrooms on each fish. Season with pepper and sprinkle with parsley, and cheese. Fold the paper over the fish to make a package. Sprinkle tops of all packages with water. Bake in moderate oven for approximately 30 minutes.

Serve hot in packages as a main course with boiled potatoes and salad. **4 servings.**

GURNARD WITH MAYONNAISE
Mayonezli Kırlangıç

2 lbs (900 gr) gurnard
6 cups (1½ liters) water
1 onion, chopped
1 cup (60 gr) parsley,
  chopped
2 bay leaves
salt and pepper to taste
MAYONNAISE
1 egg
1 teaspoon dry
  mustard
2 teaspoons sugar
1 tablespoon vinegar
1 teaspoon salt
juice of 1 lemon
¾ cup (150 ml) salad
  oil
GARNISH
6 lemon wedges
1 small carrot, cubed
  and boiled
2 tablespoons peas,
  boiled

Gut and wash fish. Bring water to a boil, add onion, parsley, bay leaves, salt, pepper and fish. Cook until fish is tender for about 20 minutes. Let cool.

Drain and transfer to a dish. Skin and bone the fish and flake it into large pieces.

Arrange the pieces on a serving platter making a fish form or use a fish-shaped platter. Spread the mayonnaise evenly over it.

Garnish with lemon wedges, carrots and peas. Serve cold as an entrée.
MAYONNAISE
Place egg, mustard, sugar, vinegar and salt into a blender. Blend for 2 minutes at high speed, pour in alternately lemon juice and olive oil without stopping the blender. Blend until a thick consistency is obtained.
VARIATION
Sea bass, turbot or halibut can replace gurnard.
6 servings.

GREY MULLET IN OLIVE OIL
Kefal Pilaki

2 lbs (900 gr) grey mullet

2 medium onions, sliced thin

½ cup (100 ml) salad oil

3 medium carrots, cubed

4 cloves garlic, chopped

3 medium potatoes, cubed

salt and pepper to taste

2 tomatoes, grated

2 lemons, sliced thin

½ cup (125 ml) water

1 cup (60 gr) parsley, chopped

juice of 1 lemon

Gut, wash fish and cut into thin slices. Set aside.

Sauté onions in oil for 2 minutes, add carrots, garlic, potatoes, salt, pepper and tomatoes. Sauté for 10 minutes.

Place fish in a heat-resistant serving dish, preferably shallow and wide. Pour vegetable mixture over. Top with lemon slices and add water. Cover and simmer for approximately 30 minutes until fish and vegetables are tender.

Garnish with chopped parsley. Serve lukewarm or at room temperature as a main course with salad. Sprinkle fish with lemon juice when eating.

VARIATION

Grey mullet can be replaced by sea bass, turbot, large bonito, bonito or gurnard.

6 servings.

POACHED BLUE FISH
Lüfer Buğulama

6 blue fish
salt
juice of 1 lemon
2 onions, cut into half
   rings
2 cloves garlic,
   chopped
¼ cup (50 ml) salad
   oil or ¼ cup (50 gr)
   butter
2 lbs (900 gr)
   tomatoes, sliced
salt and pepper to taste
1 small can
   mushrooms, sliced
¼ teaspoon sugar
1 cup (60 gr) parsley,
   chopped
2 bay leaves

Gut, wash fish and drain. Sprinkle with salt and lemon juice. Set aside.

Sauté onions and garlic in salad oil or butter, then add tomatoes, salt, pepper, mushrooms, sugar and parsley. Cook for 5-10 minutes.

Place the fish in a baking dish and spread the tomato mixture over, then add bay leaves. Cook covered for 15-20 minutes.

Serve hot as a main course with boiled potatoes and salad.

6 servings.

SARDINES IN VINE LEAVES
Asma Yaprağında Sardalya

24 sardines
salt
24 fresh vine leaves
1 cup (200 ml) olive
   oil
4 lemons, sliced and
   each slice halved
2 lemons, halved

Gut and wash sardines. Sprinkle with salt and set aside.

Put the shiny sides of vine leaves on a clean surface.

Brush with oil. Oil sardines as well. Place one sardine on the stem of each leaf. Roll up the leaves and place on a baking tray with the stem-sides up. Set aside for one hour.

Grill stuffed leaves on both sides over medium heat or charcoal about 15 minutes. Garnish with lemon slices. Open vine leaves and sprinkle fish with lemon juice when eating.

Serve hot as a main course with salad.

4 servings.

VEGETABLES
AND LEGUMES
WHITE KIDNEY BEAN
AND MEAT STEW

MEAT AND RICE STUFFING FOR VEGETABLES Etli Dolma İçi

3 large onions,
coarsely grated
¼ cup (50 gr) rice
(short grain)
1 lb (450 gr) minced
meat
salt and pepper to taste
1 cup (60 gr) parsley,
finely chopped
1 cup (60 gr) fresh
mint, finely chopped
1 cup (60 gr) dill,
finely chopped
½ cup (125 ml) water
1 tomato, grated or 1
tablespoon tomato
paste diluted in ¼
cup cold water
2 tablespoons butter

Place all the ingredients into a bowl.
Mix well and knead.
NOTE
This stuffing can be used to fill vine
leaves, cabbage leaves, tomatoes,
zucchinis, eggplants, bell peppers and
Swiss chard. Because of the different
sizes of the vegetables if there is any
left over, stuffing can be used up by
filling any of the above-mentioned
vegetables.
6 servings.

STUFFED CABBAGE LEAVES (MEAT DOLMA) Etli Lahana Dolması

3 lbs (1350 gr) white cabbage
3 cups (750 ml) boiling water
1 tablespoon tomato paste, diluted in ¼ cup cold water
2 cups (500 ml) water
2 tablespoons butter
salt to taste
meat and rice stuffing (see page 60)

Slice cabbage into two cutting towards the stem. Cut off the stem. Wash and boil cabbage in salted boiling water on high heat for 10 minutes. Drain. Cool and take out leaves. Cut off thick veins, divide leaves into palm-size sections. Put walnut-size pieces of meat and rice stuffing in the center of the cabbage leaves. Tuck in both sides and roll up.

Line a saucepan with the torn and discarded cabbage veins. Place stuffed cabbage rolls seam-side down into the saucepan.

Add tomato paste, water, dot with butter and sprinkle with salt. Place a plate upside down on top of the stuffed cabbage leaves to act as a weight. Cover and cook over low heat for about 40 minutes until cabbage is tender. Transfer stuffed cabbage leaves to a serving platter by hand carefully. Pour remaining liquid from the saucepan (about 8 tablespoons) over.

Serve hot as a main course with salad.

VARIATION

Cabbage leaves can be replaced by Swiss chard or vine leaves.

6 servings.

STUFFED ZUCCHINIS (MEAT DOLMA) Etli Kabak Dolması

12 large zucchinis
2 cups (500 ml) water
salt to taste

Scrape and wash zucchinis. Cut off stem ends. Scoop out insides and save pulp for lining the saucepan. Fill shell tightly with meat and rice stuffing. Place stuffed zucchinis side by

continued on the next page

continued from the previous page

2 *large tomatoes,*
  grated or
  2 *tablespoons tomato*
  paste, diluted in $\frac{1}{4}$
  cup cold water
2 *tablespoons butter*
1 *cup (60 gr) dill,*
  chopped
3 *cups (750 gr)*
  yoghurt
meat and rice stuffing
(see page 60)

side into a wide saucepan. Add water, salt and tomatoes and dot with butter. Place a plate upside down on top of the stuffed zucchinis to act as a weight. Cover and cook over low heat until zucchinis are tender.

Transfer stuffed zucchinis to a platter. Pour remaining gravy from the saucepan (about 8 tablespoons) over. Garnish with dill.

Serve hot with yoghurt and salad as a main course.

6 servings.

STUFFED BELL PEPPERS (MEAT DOLMA) Etli Biber Dolması

12 *small green bell*
  peppers
3 *tomatoes, quartered*
  (optional)
parsley stems
1 *tablespoon butter*
salt and pepper to taste
2 *cups (500 ml) water*
meat and rice stuffing
(see page 60)
3 *cups (750 gr) yoghurt*

Cut a thin slice from the stem end of the peppers, remove seeds and membranes, wash and save tops to act as lids. Wash. Drain upside-down.

Fill peppers with meat and rice stuffing, replace lids and cover tops either with the stems of the peppers or with the quartered tomatoes, skin-side up.

Line the bottom of a large saucepan with parsley stems, and arrange peppers upright next to each other on the parsley stems. Add salt, pepper and water. Dot with butter. Place a plate upside down on peppers. Cover and cook on lowest possible heat until peppers are tender for about 40 minutes.

Transfer stuffed peppers to a platter. Pour remaining liquid (about 8 tablespoons) from the saucepan over.

Serve hot with yoghurt and salad as a main course.

6 servings.

STUFFED TOMATOES
(MEAT DOLMA) Etli Domates Dolması

12 large tomatoes
1½ cups (375 ml)
  water
3 tablespoons butter
salt and pepper to taste
meat and rice stuffing
(see page 60)
3 cups (750 gr)
  yoghurt

Wash tomatoes. Slice off the tops and keep them for lids. Scoop out inside of tomatoes with a spoon. Save the pulp for lining the saucepan. Fill the tomatoes with meat and rice stuffing. Cover with their lids and place stuffed tomatoes upright into a tomato pulp lined saucepan. Add water. Dot tomatoes with butter. Sprinkle with salt and pepper. Place a plate upside down on top of the stuffed tomatoes to act as a weight. Cover. Simmer over low heat until tomatoes are cooked for about 30-40 minutes.

Transfer stuffed tomatoes to a serving platter. Pour remaining liquid (about 8 tablespoons) from the saucepan over.

Serve hot with yoghurt and salad as a main course.

6 servings.

SPINACH WITH MINCED MEAT
Kıymalı Ispanak

2 lbs (900 gr) spinach *⅓ cup (70 gr)* *uncooked rice* *1 large onion, grated*	Cut off spinach roots. Wash and drain spinach. Chop the spinach finely and set aside. Wash rice several times in hot water. Set aside.

2 tablespoons butter
½ lb (225 gr) minced
  beef
2 tablespoons tomato
  paste, diluted in
¼ cup cold water, or 2
  large tomatoes,
  grated
1 teaspoon sugar
salt and pepper to taste
1 cup (250 ml) hot
  water
3 cups (750 gr)
  yoghurt

Sauté onion in butter until soft and golden. Add meat. Cover and cook over low heat until meat releases its moisture and reabsorbs it. Add tomatoes, sugar, salt, pepper and ½ cup water, simmer for 15 minutes.

Place spinach in a big saucepan. Cover with meat mixture and rice. Pour ½ cup hot water over. Cook covered on medium heat until rice and spinach are cooked and most of the liquid is absorbed. Hot water may be added if necessary.

Serve hot with yoghurt as a second course after a light main dish.

4 servings.

WHITE KIDNEY BEAN AND MEAT
STEW Etli Kuru Fasulye

2 medium onions,
  grated
2 tablespoons butter
1 lb (450 gr) beef or
  lamb cubes
2 tablespoons tomato
  paste, diluted in ¼
  cup cold water
2 tomatoes, cubed
3 cups (600 gr) dried
  white beans, soaked
  overnight in salted
  lukewarm water
8 cups (2 liters)
  hot water
salt and pepper to taste
2 tablespoons paprika
2 green bell peppers,
  thinly sliced

Sauté onions lightly in butter. Add meat and sauté for 10 more minutes. Cover and cook over low heat until the meat releases its moisture and reabsorbs it. Add tomato paste and tomatoes. Stir and boil for 5 minutes. Set aside.

Boil the soaked beans in 4 cups of fresh water until they are tender. Strain, then place them in a large saucepan. Add meat mixture, salt, pepper, paprika, bell peppers and 4 cups of hot water. Cover. Cook over medium heat for about half an hour until the beans have some gravy.

Serve hot as a main course with pilaf and pickles.
VARIATION
Meat can be replaced by sausages, salami, bacon or minced meat.
8 servings.

POTATOES WITH MEAT
Etli Patates

2 onions, chopped
2 tablespoons butter
1 lb (450 gr) lamb or
    beef cubes or minced
    meat
8 large potatoes,
    peeled, diced
$\frac{1}{2}$ cup (100 ml) salad
    oil
4 tomatoes, skinned,
    seeded, sliced
3 cups (750 ml) hot
    water
salt and pepper to taste
6 pepperones or 3
    green bell peppers,
    seeded and sliced
1 teaspoon paprika

Sauté onions in butter. Add meat and sauté for 15 minutes. Cover and cook over low heat until the meat releases its moisture and reabsorbs it.

Fry potatoes lightly in salad oil. Set aside.

Place meat mixture, tomatoes, water, salt and pepper in a big saucepan. Cover and simmer. Add potatoes and pepperones. Simmer until the meat and potatoes are tender and the dish has a thick gravy. Sprinkle with paprika.

Serve as a main course with salad and Turkish bread.

4 servings.

LENTIL AND MEAT STEW
Etli Mercimek

1½ cups (270 gr) green
lentils, soaked
overnight
2 large onions, grated
3 tablespoons butter
1 lb (450 gr) lamb or
beef cubes or minced
meat
1 tablespoon tomato
paste, diluted in ¼
cup cold water
3 carrots, cubed
salt and pepper to taste
4 cups (1 liter) hot
water

Wash and drain lentils. Place into a saucepan and set aside.

Sauté onions lightly in butter. Add meat and sauté for about 15 minutes then cover and cook on low heat until the meat releases its moisture and reabsorbs it, and becomes tender. Add tomato paste. Stir once, then add the meat mixture, carrots, salt and pepper to lentils. Add hot water. Cover. Cook over medium heat until lentils are tender, the liquid is mostly absorbed and yet some gravy is left.

Serve hot as a main course with pilaf and salad.

8 servings.

EGGPLANT PURÉE
Patlıcan Beğendi

2 large eggplants
*2 tablespoons lemon
 juice*
2 tablespoons butter
2 tablespoons flour
1½ cups (375 ml) milk
salt and pepper to taste
*4 tablespoons gruyère
 or parmesan cheese,
 grated*

Pierce the eggplants with a fork. Place them in a pan over an open flame or on a high gas flame or on charcoal and cook them for half an hour, turning them often until the skin blisters on all sides and the eggplant becomes soft. Cool. Set aside.

Slice the eggplants into two lengthways. Scoop out the pulp, squeeze out all the moisture and mash with a fork on a wooden board. Place the eggplant pulp into a bowl, add lemon juice and set aside.

Place butter in a saucepan, add flour and cook over low heat stirring constantly for 5 minutes, add cold milk and continue stirring for 10 minutes. Add salt and pepper. Mix eggplants together with this mixture. Add cheese and mash until it turns· into a paste.

Serve hot as a side dish with stewed meat or baked or fried chicken.
8 servings.

EGGPLANT WITH MINCED MEAT
Karnıyarık

6 eggplants, long and fat

1 cup (200 ml) salad oil

2 large onions, grated

3 tablespoons butter

1 lb (450 gr) minced beef

2 tomatoes, grated, or 1 tablespoon tomato paste, diluted in $\frac{1}{4}$ cup cold water

$\frac{1}{2}$ cup (30 gr) parsley, chopped

salt and pepper to taste

1 tomato, sliced into 6 wedges

3 green bell peppers, seeded and sliced into 2

1 cup (250 ml) hot water

Cut off the stems of the eggplants. Peel eggplants in strips. Sauté eggplants in salad oil until golden brown. Slit eggplants open lengthways but not quite to the end, so that they remain in one piece. Place them side by side in a single layer open side up in a baking dish.

Sauté onions in butter until lightly browned. Add meat and sauté for 10 minutes, then cover and cook over low heat until the meat releases its moisture and reabsorbs it. Add grated tomatoes. Cook for 10 more minutes then add parsley, salt and pepper.

Stuff the eggplants with the meat mixture, enlarging the openings by hand. Place a slice of tomato and half a green pepper on top of each eggplant. Add water. Bake covered in a moderate oven for 30 minutes.

Serve hot as a main course with pilaf.

6 servings.

CELERY ROOTS WITH LEMON AND EGG SAUCE Terbiyeli Kereviz

5 celery roots
4 cups (1 liter) water
2 tablespoons flour
1 lemon, quartered
2 whole onions
salt to taste
2 tablespoons butter
SAUCE
2 eggs
2 tablespoons lemon juice

Peel and wash the celery roots. Cut into ½ - inch (1.5 cm) slices. Pour 2 cups of water into a bowl, mix in flour, drop in lemon pieces. Put celery in the floured water to prevent discoloration and to obtain gravy with thick consistency. Transfer celery into a saucepan with water and flour, remove lemon pieces, add onions, 2 cups of water, salt and butter, cook over low heat until celery roots are tender and most of the water is absorbed. Remove onions. Mix eggs and lemon juice in a bowl, add 1 cup celery gravy from the saucepan, stir. Pour this mixture over the hot celery roots, stir once and serve immediately as a side dish with meat.

6 servings.

CELERY ROOTS IN OLIVE OIL
Zeytinyağlı Kereviz

2 lbs (900 gr) celery roots
4 cups (1 liter) water
juice of 1 lemon
2 onions, grated or 10 pearl onions
½ cup (100 ml) olive oil or salad oil
4 cups (1 liter) hot water
1 tablespoon lemon juice
2 carrots, diced
2 potatoes, diced
1 cup (100 gr) peas
1 tablespoon sugar
salt to taste
½ cup (30 gr) dill, chopped

Peel the outer skin of the celery roots. Wash, drain and cut into ½ - inch (1.5 cm) slices.

Cook for 15 minutes in boiling water with lemon juice. Drain and set aside.

Sauté onions in olive oil for 2 minutes, add hot water, lemon juice, celery roots, carrots, potatoes, peas, sugar and salt. Cover and cook over high heat for 15 minutes, lower heat and let it simmer for another 15 minutes until vegetables are tender and there is some liquid left. Cool.

Transfer celery roots to a serving platter. Pour potatoes, carrots, peas and the liquid from the pan over the celery roots.

Garnish with dill. Serve as an entrée.
6 servings.

GREEN BEANS IN OLIVE OIL
Zeytinyağlı Taze Fasulye

2 lbs (900 gr) green
  beans
½ cup (100 ml) olive
  oil or salad oil
2 onions, grated
salt to taste
1 teaspoon sugar
2 medium tomatoes,
  cut into quarters
4 cups (1 liter) water

Top, tail and string the beans and
wash. Place beans into a saucepan,
add olive oil, onions, salt, sugar and
tomatoes.
  Cover the lid, cook over very high
heat for 3 minutes. Lift the saucepan
and hold it together with the lid by
the hands and shake. Replace the pan
on the stove. Repeat this process 3-4
times until the beans turn bright
green. Add boiling water. Turn heat to
medium and cook until beans are
tender and the water is mostly
absorbed. Pour the beans onto a
serving platter and serve cold as a
second course or as an appetizer.
6 servings.

EGGPLANTS IN OLIVE OIL
İmam Bayıldı

6 medium eggplants
1 cup (200 ml) salad oil
6 small onions, sliced in rings
$\frac{1}{4}$ cup (50 ml) olive oil
6 medium tomatoes, skinned, seeded and sliced
6 cloves garlic, sliced lengthways into 2
1 cup (60 gr) parsley, chopped
salt to taste
1$\frac{1}{2}$ teaspoons sugar
3 cups (750 ml) water

Cut off the stems of the eggplants. Peel eggplants in strips. Sauté eggplants in 1 cup salad oil until golden brown for better taste (for a lighter dish frying can be eliminated).

Slit open eggplants lenghtways leaving both ends uncut. Place them side by side in a single layer open sides up in a shallow and large saucepan. Set aside.

Sauté onions in $\frac{1}{4}$ cup oil until they are soft and golden brown. Add tomatoes, garlic, parsley and salt. Simmer for 15 minutes. Remove from heat. Stuff the eggplants with this mixture.

Add $\frac{1}{4}$ cup olive oil, sugar, salt and water. Cover and cook over medium heat for about an hour until the eggplants are tender. Transfer gently to a serving platter.

Serve cold as an appetizer.

6 servings.

RICE DOLMA STUFFING IN OLIVE OIL
Zeytinyağlı Dolma İçi

1¼ cups (250 gr) rice
1 cup (200 ml) olive oil or salad oil
1⅔ lbs (750 gr) onions, grated
3 tablespoons pine nuts
salt to taste
2 tablespoons sugar
3 tablespoons currant
1¼ cups (312 ml) hot water
1 tablespoon allspice
1 teaspoon cinnamon
pepper to taste
1 bunch of parsley, chopped

Soak rice in plenty of salted warm water, leave until water cools. Wash and drain.

Heat olive oil or salad oil in a saucepan. Sauté onions and pine nuts for 5 minutes. Add rice and cook for another 5 minutes, stirring constantly. Add salt, sugar and currants. Stir together and pour in hot water, stir once. Cover and cook over very low heat until water is absorbed, about 25 minutes.

Add allspice, cinnamon, pepper, parsley, mint and dill, stir and cook for 1 minute. Remove from heat and cool.

74

1 bunch of mint leaves, finely chopped
1 bunch of dill, chopped

NOTE

The amount of olive oil can be adjusted to individual taste.

This stuffing can be used to fill vine leaves, cabbage leaves, tomatoes, bell peppers and eggplants. Because of the different sizes of the vegetables if there is any leftover, stuffing can be finished by using any of the above-mentioned vegetables.

6 servings.

STUFFED CABBAGE LEAVES IN OLIVE OIL (RICE DOLMA)
Zeytinyağlı Lahana Dolması

3½ lbs (1575 gr) white cabbage
1¼ cups (312 ml) hot water
salt to taste
rice dolma stuffing (see page 74)
GARNISH
2 lemons cut into wedges

Wash and place cabbage core up in the boiling water. Boil for 5 minutes, drain and cool. Remove leaves with care.

Cut leaves into sections of about 4 inches (10 cm) long, 6 inches (15 cm) wide discarding veins and cores. Line the saucepan with discarded leaves.

Take sectioned cabbage leaf in your palm. Place rice stuffing on the stem end. Tuck in sides. Roll towards the end. Place stuffed cabbage leaves next to each other seam-side downward in the saucepan in one, two or three layers depending on the size of the saucepan.

Sprinkle salt over. Cover with a plate for weight. Add hot water, put the lid on and simmer on a low heat for about an hour. Remove from heat, cool while still covered. Refrigerate overnight. Transfer to a serving platter. Decorate with lemon wedges.

Serve cold as an entrée or hors d'oeuvre.

10 servings.

STUFFED VINE LEAVES IN OLIVE OIL (RICE DOLMA)

Zeytinyağlı Yaprak Dolması

36 fresh or preserved
  vine leaves
1¼ cups (312 ml) hot
  water
salt to taste
rice dolma stuffing
  (see page 74)
GARNISH
2 lemons cut into
  wedges

Boil vine leaves in 2 cups of boiling water for 2 minutes, drain. Trim stems and veins from leaves. Pat dry on paper toweling.

Line saucepan with torn vine leaves. Hold single leaf, vein-side up in palm of hand. Place about 1 tablespoon of the rice filling on stem end of leaf. Tuck in sides, fold end over filling, roll. Place seam-side down in saucepan. Place all the stuffed vine leaves side by side in one or two layers depending on the size of saucepan. Sprinkle salt over them.

Pour 1¼ cups hot water over. Cover with a plate for weight. Put the lid on. Simmer covered over low heat for about an hour until vine leaves are tender. Let cool in the saucepan before transferring to a serving dish lined with green salad leaves. Refrigerate overnight.

Garnish with lemon wedges. Serve cold as an entrée or hors d'oeuvre.

NOTE

Boiled Swiss chard leaves with their stems removed can replace vine leaves.

6 servings.

STUFFED TOMATOES IN OLIVE OIL (RICE DOLMA)

Zeytinyağlı Domates Dolması

*12 large half-ripe
  tomatoes*
*1 cup (250 ml) hot
  water*
salt to taste
*rice dolma stuffing
(see page 74)*
GARNISH
*2 lemons cut into
  wedges*

Slice tops of tomatoes through, but do not sever. Sliced tops are to serve as covers. Scoop out insides with a small spoon. Set aside the pulp of 6 tomatoes.

Stuff tomatoes with rice filling, pressing down. Do not overstuff. Cover with tomato tops. Line the saucepan with pulp from 6 tomatoes and place stuffed tomatoes top side up, next to each other. Pour over hot water and sprinkle with salt. Cover with a plate for weight. Put the lid on. Let pan simmer over low heat until water is absorbed and tomatoes are cooked.

Remove from heat, cool while still covered. Transfer to a serving platter. Garnish with lemon wedges. Refrigerate overnight. Serve cold as an entrée or hors d'oeuvre.
12 servings.

STUFFED BELL PEPPERS IN OLIVE OIL (RICE DOLMA)
Zeytinyağlı Biber Dolması

*12 large green bell
  peppers*
*6 small tomatoes,
  sliced into 2
  (optional)*
*1¼ cups (312 ml)
  water or juice of
  fresh tomatoes*
salt to taste
rice dolma stuffing
(see page 74)
GARNISH
*2 lemons cut into
  wedges*

Cut a thin slice from stem end of peppers, remove seeds and membranes, wash and save tops to serve as covers (tomato halves can also be used as covers if a more colorful presentation is preferred). Set aside.

Stuff bell peppers with rice filling. Press it down. Don't overstuff. Cover with tomato or pepper tops.

Line a large saucepan with the pulp of tomatoes. Place stuffed peppers upright side by side. Pour in 1¼ cups of hot water or tomato juice. Sprinkle salt over. Cover with a plate for weight. Put the lid on and cook over low heat until water is absorbed and peppers are cooked. Cool while still covered. Transfer to a serving platter.

Refrigerate overnight serve cold as an entrée or hors d'oeuvre.

12 servings

STUFFED EGGPLANTS IN OLIVE OIL (RICE DOLMA)
Zeytinyağlı Patlıcan Dolması

6 large and long
  eggplants
1¼ cups (312 ml) hot
  water
salt to taste
rice dolma stuffing
(see page 74)
GARNISH
2 lemons cut into
  wedges

Cut off each eggplant about 1 inch (2.5 cm) from stem end. Save stems and scoop out pulp leaving ¼ - inch (1 cm) thick shells. Mince 1 cup of pulp, sprinkle with salt, wash after half an hour, drain, squeeze dry and mix with the rice stuffing. Stuff eggplant shells with this mixture. Cover with stems. Line the saucepan with leftover eggplant pulp. Lay eggplants side by side. Pour hot water over and add salt. Cover with a plate for weight. Put the lid on. Cook covered on a very low heat until the eggplants are cooked and water is absorbed. Remove from heat, cool while still covered. Place stuffed eggplants on a serving dish cutting them each into 2 or 3 pieces.

Garnish with lemon wedges. Refrigerate overnight. Serve cold as an entrée or hors d'oeuvre.
12 servings.

ARTICHOKES IN OLIVE OIL
Zeytinyağlı Enginar

6 large artichokes
2 cups (500 ml) cold water
3 tablespoons flour
juice of 2 lemons
3 onions, sliced in rings
½ cup (100 ml) olive oil or salad oil
1 large carrot, diced
1 large potato, diced
½ cup (50 gr) peas
1 tablespoon sugar
salt to taste
1 cup (125 ml) hot water
½ cup (30 gr) dill, chopped

Remove the leaves of artichokes until the hearts are exposed. Scrape the hairy surface of the hearts with a knife. Trim the bottom of the hearts. When cutting the stems make sure you leave about 2 inches (5 cm) on the bottom of the hearts. Set aside.

Pour cold water into a bowl, sprinkle with flour and add lemon juice. Drop artichokes in it to prevent discoloration.

Sauté onions in olive oil or salad oil in a saucepan for a few minutes. Add carrot and sauté for another 5 minutes. Then add potato, peas, sugar, salt and artichokes. Add water. Cook covered over high heat for 10 minutes. Lower heat and simmer for about 45 minutes until artichokes are tender and have some gravy. Cool.

Transfer artichokes, stem side up in a serving platter. Pour vegetables and the gravy over.

Garnish with dill. Serve cold as an entrée.

6 servings.

FRIED ZUCCHINIS
Kabak Kızartması

4 zucchinis
1 cup (250 ml) beer
1½ cups (150 gr) flour
1 tablespoon ketchup
salt to taste
salad oil (about 1½
    inches - 4 cm. deep in
    the frying pan)
SAUCE (optional)
2 cups (500 gr)
    yoghurt
2 cloves garlic, crushed

Scrape and wash zucchinis and cut in very thin slices - lengthways.

Pour beer into a bowl, add flour, ketchup and salt, mix well with a fork for coating. Set aside.

Heat oil in a heavy frying pan. Dredge zucchinis in the coating mixture. Fry both sides on high heat until zucchinis are crisp. Transfer to a serving platter.

Mix yoghurt and garlic together with a fork and transfer to a small serving bowl.

Serve fried zucchinis with yoghurt and garlic sauce as an appetizer.
NOTE
Zucchinis can also be deep fried.
8 servings.

FRIED CARROTS
Havuç Kızartması

6 large carrots
1 cup (250 ml) beer
1½ cups (150 gr) flour
1 tablespoon ketchup
salt to taste
salad oil (about 1½
    inch - 4 cm deep in the
    frying pan)
SAUCE (optional)
2 cups (500 gr)
    yoghurt
2 cloves garlic, crushed

Scrape and wash carrots. Cut into very thin slices lengthways. Set aside.

Place 1 cup of beer in a bowl, add flour gradually, add ketchup and salt mix well stirring with a fork for coating. Set aside.

Heat oil in a heavy frying pan. Dredge carrots in the coating mixture. Fry both sides on high heat until a crust is formed. Transfer fried carrots to a serving platter.

Mix yoghurt and garlic together with a fork, transfer to a small serving bowl.

Serve hot with yoghurt and garlic sauce as an appetizer.
NOTE
Carrots can also be deep fried.
8 servings.

KAŞAR
CHEESE

YUFKA

KAYMAK

WHITE
CHEESE

INDIGENOUS TURKISH INGREDIENTS

PILAFS, BÖREK, PASTA DISHES, BREAD
RAVIOLI ALLA TURCA

ORIENTAL RICE
İç Pilav

2 cups (400 gr) rice
  (long grain)
2 tablespoons salt
4 cups (1 liter) boiling
  water for soaking
  rice
3 tablespoons butter
3 tablespoons pine
  nuts
1 onion, chopped
3 cups (750 ml) water
  and chicken broth
4 tablespoons currants
salt and pepper to taste
1 tablespoon sugar
$\frac{1}{4}$ lb (112.5 gr) chicken
  or lamb liver, diced
  (optional)
1 tablespoon allspice
$\frac{1}{2}$ teaspoon cinnamon
$\frac{1}{2}$ cup (30 gr) dill

Place rice into a bowl with 2
teaspoons salt and pour boiling water
over, stir and let it stand until water
cools. Drain. Wash well under cold
water, drain again. Set aside.

Melt 2 tablespoons butter in a
saucepan, add pine nuts and onion.
Sauté until they are light brown. Add
rice and stir for 5 minutes. Then add
the chicken broth and water mixture,
currants, salt, pepper and sugar.

Sauté diced liver in 1 tablespoon
butter and add to the rice mixture.
Cook over medium heat until water is
absorbed by the rice. Then add
allspice, cinnamon and dill, and leave
the saucepan on very low heat over an
asbestos pad for about 10-15 minutes.
Turn heat off, uncover, place a clean
paper or a napkin over the saucepan,
replace the cover and let it stand at
least for half an hour before serving.
Stir very gently before serving.

Serve as a side dish with roast
chicken or turkey or shish kebab.
8 servings.

PILAF WITH TOMATOES
Domatesli Pilav

*1 cup (200 gr) rice
(long grain)
2 tablespoons salt
3 cups (750 ml)
boiling water
1 tablespoon butter
2 cups (500 ml) tomato
juice
salt to taste*

Place rice into a bowl with 2 teaspoons salt and pour boiling water over, stir and let it stand until water cools. Drain, wash well under cold water, drain again. Set aside.

Place butter, tomato juice and salt in a saucepan and boil, add rice, stir once, cover and boil over high heat for 2 minutes. Turn heat to low and put an asbestos pad under the saucepan, cook until rice absorbs all the liquid. Turn heat off, uncover, place a clean paper or a napkin over the saucepan, replace the cover and let it stand for at least half an hour before serving. A wooden spoon is recommended to transfer rice pilaf from saucepan to serving plate.

Serve with meat or chicken as a side dish.

4 servings.

PILAF WITH MUSSELS
Midyeli Pilav

1¼ cups (300 gr) rice
(long grain)
2 teaspoons salt
4 cups (1 liter) boiling
water
2 medium onions,
grated
2 tablespoons pine
nuts
½ cup (100 ml) olive
oil
1 large tomato, grated
salt to taste
1 teaspoon sugar
2 tablespoons currants
50 mussels, shelled,
washed and
drained
2 cups (500 ml) water
1 tablespoon allspice
pepper to taste
½ cup (30 gr) dill,
chopped

Place rice into a bowl with 2 teaspoons salt and pour boiling water over. Stir and let it stand until water cools. Drain, wash well under cold water, drain again.

Sauté onions and pine nuts in olive oil in a frying pan until they become light brown. Add rice, stir for 2 minutes then add tomato, salt, sugar, currants, mussels and 2 cups boiling water. Cover and cook over high heat for 5 minutes and then turn heat to low and put an asbestos pad under the saucepan, cover and cook until rice absorbs all the water and becomes fluffy, turn heat off. Uncover, and add allspice and pepper. Remove from heat, stir once or twice very gently and place a clean paper or a napkin over the saucepan. Replace the cover.

Transfer to a platter and serve at room temperature. Garnish with dill. Traditionally this is served after the main dish. It can also be served as an entrée.

NOTE
Curry powder may replace allspice.
8 servings.

POUNDED WHEAT PILAF
Bulgur Pilavı

1 cup (160 gr) plain bulgur or pounded wheat
2 tablespoons butter
1 large onion, grated
3 pepperones, seeded, chopped
salt and pepper to taste
1 cup (250 ml) meat stock or chicken broth
1 cup (250 ml) tomato juice
½ cup (30 gr) parsley, chopped

Wash and drain bulgur. Place butter, onion, pepperones, salt and pepper into a saucepan, sauté, stirring for 2 minutes, pour in chicken broth and tomato juice, bring to a boil. Add bulgur and stir once. Turn heat to low and cook over an asbestos pad until bulgur absorbs all the liquid. Remove from heat and add parsley. Stir once with a wooden spoon. Cover saucepan with a clean paper or a napkin. Replace cover. Let it stand for an hour. Serve hot with any meat dish. **4 servings.**

WHITE PILAF
Beyaz Pilav

*1 cup (200 gr) rice
(long grain)*
2 teaspoons salt
*4 cups (1 liter) boiling
water*
*2 cups (500 ml)
chicken broth*
1½ tablespoons butter
salt to taste
*2 tablespoons pine
nuts*
2 tablespoons currants

Place rice into a bowl with 2 teaspoons salt and pour boiling water over, stir and let it stand until water cools. Drain, wash well under cold water, drain again.

Place chicken broth, butter, salt, pine nuts and currants into a saucepan, bring to a boil. Add rice and stir once.

Turn heat on low and put an asbestos pad under the saucepan, cover and cook until rice absorbs all the water and becomes fluffy. Turn heat off, uncover, place a clean paper or a napkin over the saucepan, replace the cover and let it stand for at least half an hour before serving. Stir and serve hot. A wooden spoon is recommended to transfer rice pilaf from saucepan to serving plate. Serve with meat or chicken as a side dish. **4 servings.**

RAVIOLI ALLA TURCA
Mantı

FILLING
½ lb (225 gr) minced
   beef
1 large onion, grated
salt and pepper to taste
¼ *cup (15 gr) parsley,*
   finely chopped
DOUGH
2 cups (200 gr) flour
1 teaspoon salt
½ *cup (125 ml) water*
1 egg
1½ *cups (150 gr) flour*
   for rolling out the
   pastry
FOR BOILING
6 cups (1½ liters) water
   or chicken broth
1 teaspoon salt

Mix meat, onion, salt, pepper and parsley in a bowl. Set aside.

Mix flour and 1 teaspoon salt together in a mixing bowl. Make a hollow in the middle. Pour in ½ cup water and the egg.

Mix with fingertips and knead the dough with the hands.

Place the dough preferably on a wooden floured work surface. Knead until the dough is smooth and elastic and does not stick to the hand. Cover with a napkin and set aside for 1 hour at room temperature.

Divide the dough into two. On a floured surface, knead well and shape each piece into a round ball. Cover one ball with a napkin and roll out the other with a long thin rolling pin. Wrap one edge of the pastry around the rolling pin. Roll forward pressing gently towards the ends of the pin. Flip the pastry open. Repeat this process from different edges until the pastry is $\frac{1}{16}$ inch ($\frac{1}{6}$ cm) thick. Cut with a knife into 2 x 2 - inch (5 x 5 cm) squares.

Place a teaspoon of meat filling in the center. Pick up four corners, pinching firmly and making sure all sides are sealed.

The squares can also be sealed by pinching opposite corners together and pressing the two sides forming mantı (little pastries) in triangular shapes. Roll out the second ball of dough and repeat the same process.

Put chicken broth or water into a very large saucepan. Bring to a boil.

Place mantıs carefully in the boiling water. Do not overcrowd them. Lower the heat. Occasionally stir with a

YOGHURT SAUCE
4 cups (1 kg) yoghurt
3 cloves garlic,
  (optional)
DRESSING
2 tablespoons butter,
  melted
½ teaspoon paprika

wooden spoon. The pastries rise to the surface when they are cooked - about 15 minutes. Remove with a perforated kitchen spoon to a heated serving plate, pour ½ cup liquid over from the saucepan, keep warm.

Combine yoghurt and crushed garlic, mix well. Spread this sauce over the pastries.

Melt butter in a small pan. Add paprika and stir for a few minutes. Trickle dressing over yoghurt sauce.

Serve hot as a main dish with salad.
12 servings.

SAVORY PIE
Tepsi Böreği

2 cups (200 gr) flour
1 egg
½ cup (125 ml) water
pinch of salt
½ cup (100 ml)
  vegetable oil
2 cups (200 gr) flour
  for rolling out the
  dough
PASTRY
(readymade)
6 Turkish börek
  yufkası or
12 phyllo sheets
SAUCE BETWEEN
LAYERS
⅔ cup (130 gr)
  margarine
2 cups (500 ml) milk
3 eggs
(melt margarine, add
milk, mix in eggs, stir,
set aside)
CHEESE FILLING
⅔ lb (300 gr) Turkish
  white cheese,
  crumbled or cottage
  cheese
1 bunch parsley,
  chopped
1 bunch dill, chopped
1 egg
(mix ingredients in a
bowl with a fork, set
aside)
MEAT FILLING
1 lb (450 gr) minced
  beef
2 onions, chopped
1 tablespoon butter
1 tomato, grated
salt and pepper to taste

HOW TO MAKE THE DOUGH AND
THE PIE
Sift flour over a board or marble
surface, make a hollow in the middle,
put in egg, water, salt and oil. Knead
until dough is formed. Shape into a
roll and cut into 10 slices. Cover
with a damp napkin. Set aside for
half an hour. Spread flour
over the board. Roll out each piece,
brush with oil and fold into three.
Allow to stand for another half hour.
Roll out each piece into a round
shape of about 12 inches (30 cm) in
diameter, except for one which will
line a well-buttered baking dish,
preferably non-stick, and hangs over
the sides of the tray. Over this layer
spread margarine, milk and egg sauce.
Place a 12-inch (30 cm) sheet over,
spread sauce, and repeat this
alternately until half of the dough is
finished. Spread the filling over
(cheese, meat or spinach).
  Repeat alternate layering. Brush the
top with margarine. Set aside for an
hour. Cut into squares of desired
dimensions before baking. Bake in
moderate oven until golden brown.
Remove from the oven. Let it cool.
Turn upside down into a serving dish.
HOW TO MAKE BÖREK WITH
READYMADE YUFKA
Use a 12-inch (30 cm) round baking
dish. If phyllo pastry is used, prefer a
12 x 14 - inch (16 x 30 cm). Butter
the dish. Line with one sheet of yufka
pastry, overhanging on the sides.
Spread egg, milk and margarine sauce
over the pastry. Lay another sheet of
pastry over, this time as big as the
dish. Spread the sauce. Repeat

(cook all ingredients in a saucepan until meat is tender and tomato juice is absorbed, set aside)
SPINACH FILLING
(cooked)
2 lbs (900 gr) spinach
2 onions, grated
2 tablespoons butter
salt and pepper to taste
(Cut off the roots of the spinach, boil the leaves, strain and chop. Sauté onions with butter, add chopped spinach, salt and pepper to taste. Cook for 15 minutes)

alternate layering until half of the pastry is used. Spread the desired filling over cheese, meat or spinach. Repeat alternate layers until the remaining pastry is finished. Brush top with margarine. Set aside for an hour. Cut in individual portions as desired. Bake in moderate oven until top is golden brown. Remove from the oven. Let it cool. Turn it upside down onto a serving dish.

VARIATION

Instead of layers, individual pies can be made by rolling out squares to desired dimensions. Put filling in the center and fold in sides, wet the edges with cold water to seal. Brush top with margarine.

Serve hot as an entrée.

8 servings.

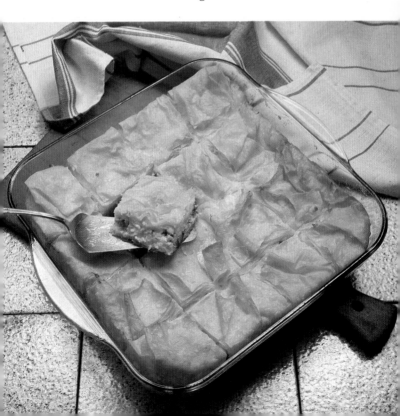

CHICKEN AND PILAF IN PASTRY
Yufkalı Pilav

½ cup (100 gr) butter,
 melted
1½ large yufka sheets
 or 6 sheets of phyllo
 pastry
white pilaf cooked
with 2 cups (400 gr)
rice (see page 91)
3 medium carrots,
 diced, boiled and
 salted
1 cup (100 gr) peas,
 drained and salted
1 cup (60 gr) dill,
 finely chopped
2 lbs (900 gr) chicken,
 boiled and cut into
 bite sizes and salted

Butter a 12 - inch (30 cm) round oven dish, preferably non-stick. Line the dish with one sheet of pastry hanging over the rim of the dish. Brush butter over the surface generously. Cut 2 pieces from the ½ yufka as big as the oven dish. Place one of them over the first layer. Brush the surface with butter, and save the other to top the dish.

If phyllo pastry is used butter a 2 x 14 - inch (16 x 30 cm) oven dish, arrange 4 sheets to line the dish. They have to be on top of each other in the dish and overhang in 4 directions. For the second and top layers use 2 more sheets.

Arrange rice, carrots, peas, dill and chicken meat in layers in the pastry lined dish. Cover top with the remaining pastry, brush with butter. Fold in overhanging first layer of pastry to cover and seal the rice and chicken mixture. Butter top. Bake in moderate oven until top and bottom are golden brown. Remove from oven. Put aside for 5 minutes. Turn it upside down onto a round serving plate. Cut the crust the way pies are cut.

Serve hot as a main course with salad.
8 servings.

TURKISH BREAD
Ekmek

3 tablespoons Turkish
  Pakmaya or
  compressed yeast,
  crumbled
½ cup (125 ml)
  lukewarm water
3 tablespoons sugar
2½ cups (250 gr) flour
1½ teaspoons salt

Place yeast into a bowl, add ¼ cup lukewarm water and allow 5-10 minutes for the yeast to soften. Pour the remaining ¼ cup water over. Add sugar, flour and salt.

Since different flours vary in the amount of moisture they can absorb, it is not generally possible to give the exact amount of flour required. Sufficient flour should be used to make the dough stiff enough to knead and to keep it from sticking to the hands. All the necessary flour should be added at the time of mixing.

Combine all the ingredients and turn the dough out onto a lightly floured board. Curve your fingers over the dough and push down with heel part of palm. Give dough a quarter turn, fold over and push down again. Knead until the dough is smooth, satiny and elastic, for about 15 minutes. Cover with a cloth and leave to rise in a warm place for 1½ hours. It rises best at a temperature between 80°-85° F (26°-29°C). After the first rising knead lightly for 2 minutes brush dough with water, and allow to rise for a second time for about 15 minutes. Press dough gently with fingers. If impression remains dough has risen sufficiently. Dough should be allowed to double in bulk.

Shape dough with hands into a long and oval loaf and place onto a greased pan. On top of the loaf make a few impressions with a knife to allow circulation of hot air. Bake in moderate oven set to 300°F (150°C) for about 30 minutes. Allow to cool before serving.
Makes 1 loaf.

DESSERTS
PUMPKIN DESSERT

PUMPKIN DESSERT
Kabak Tatlısı

4½ lbs (2 kg)
  pumpkin, peeled
5½ cups (1 kg) sugar
1 cup (100 gr)
  walnuts, grated

Pare and cut pumpkins into slices. Wash. Cut each slice into 1 - inch (2.5 cm) squares. Place them into a large saucepan - sprinkling sugar between layers. Cook over medium heat for more than an hour until pumpkin is very tender and syrup is formed.

Transfer to a serving plate with the syrup. Allow 2 hours before serving for pumpkin to absorb most of the syrup. When serving pour over a little syrup with a spoon from the serving plate.

Garnish with grated walnuts.
NOTE
This dessert keeps for 2-3 days at room temperature.
16 servings.

CREAM-STUFFED APRICOTS
Kaymaklı Kuru Kayısı

1 lb (450 gr) dried
  apricots
2½ cups (450 gr)
  sugar
3 cups (750 ml) water
1 teaspoon lemon juice
1 lb (450 gr) heavy
  whipped cream or
  kaymak (thick
  Turkish cream)
  (see page 84)
¾ cup (150 gr)
  pistachio nuts,
  grated

Soak apricots in cold water overnight. Drain. Heat sugar and water together over medium heat for 10 minutes. Add apricots and cook until apricots are tender and water becomes syrup. Add lemon juice, cook for 1 minute. Remove from heat. Transfer apricots with a perforated spoon to a plate. Allow to cool.

Half open the apricots. Fill the inside with kaymak or whipped cream. Arrange apricots side by side on a platter. Over the apricots, gradually pour as much syrup as they can absorb

Garnish with grated pistachio nuts.
12 servings.

NOAH'S PUDDING
Aşure

$\frac{3}{4}$ cup (120 gr) whole
  wheat
$\frac{1}{3}$ cup (70 gr) chick
  peas
$\frac{1}{3}$ cup (70 gr) dried
  white beans
9 cups (2$\frac{1}{4}$ liters) water
1 tablespoon rice
1$\frac{1}{2}$ cups (270 gr)
  sugar
$\frac{1}{3}$ cup (40 gr) sultanas
10 dried apricots
6 dried figs
10 chestnuts, boiled,
  skinned, chopped
1 teaspoon rose water
  (optional)
GARNISH
2 tablespoons
  cinnamon (optional)
1 cup (100 gr)
  walnuts
1 cup (100 gr)
  hazelnuts
1 tablespoon currants
1 tablespoon pine nuts
1 cup (100 gr)
  blanched almonds
seeds of one
  pomegranate

Soak wheat, chick peas and dried beans overnight in separate bowls. Wash and drain. Boil wheat, chick peas and dried beans separately in plenty of water until very tender. Remove from heat and drain and save the liquid. Skin chick peas.

Put wheat, beans and chick peas into a big and heavy saucepan. Measure the saved liquid and add water until it becomes 9 cups. Pour over the mixture. Add rice, bring to a boil, lower heat and simmer for 1 hour. Add sugar, simmer for 30 minutes.

Wash and soak sultanas, apricots and figs in hot water for 5 minutes. Drain and quarter apricots, chop figs into small pieces. Add sultanas, apricots, figs and chestnuts to the wheat, beans, chick peas, rice and sugar mixture and stir. Simmer for another 15 minutes stirring constantly. Remove from heat, pour rose water over. Stir.

Transfer to a serving bowl or individual dessert bowls. Sprinkle with cinnamon. Garnish with walnuts, hazelnuts, currants, pine nuts, blanched almonds and pomegrenate seeds.

12 servings.

ALMOND PUDDING
Keşkül

1 cup (100 gr)
  almonds
3 cups (750 ml) milk
1 cup (180 gr) sugar
$\frac{1}{4}$ teaspoon vanilla
$\frac{1}{3}$ cup (35 gr)
  cornstarch
$\frac{1}{2}$ cup (125 ml) cold
  water
GARNISH
1 tablespoon almonds,
  ground
1 tablespoon unsalted
  pistachio nuts,
  ground
1 tablespoon coconut,
  ground
6 maraschino cherries

Boil almonds, blanche and place into a blender. Add 1 cup of milk and blend for 5 minutes. Transfer to a saucepan. Add 2 cups of milk and bring this mixture to a boil. Add sugar and vanilla, boil for 10 minutes while stirring constantly. Remove from heat.

Dissolve cornstarch in $\frac{1}{2}$ cup of cold water. Add this to the almond, milk and sugar mixture and cook for another 10 minutes stirring constantly. Cool and pour into individual serving dishes.

Refrigerate for 2 hours. Garnish with almonds, pistachio nuts, coconut and maraschino cherries.
6 servings.

SEMOLINA HALVA
İrmik Helvası

SYRUP
2½ cups (625 ml) milk
2½ cups (625 ml)
   water
2 cups (360 gr) sugar

1 cup (200 gr) butter
   or margarine
3 cups (480 gr)
   semolina
3 tablespoons pine
   nuts or blanched
   almonds
1 cup (180 gr) sugar
3 tablespoons
   cinnamon (optional)
3 tablespoons
   powdered sugar
   (optional)

Place milk, water and sugar into a saucepan. Bring to a boil. Set aside. Keep steaming hot.

Stir butter, semolina and pine nuts or almonds in a heavy saucepan. Stir constantly on low heat with a wooden spoon until pine nuts or almonds turn light brown for about half an hour. Make sure not to burn the semolina.

Pour steaming hot milk and sugar syrup over hot semolina mixture. Stir once. Cover and let it simmer occasionally stirring until it absorbs all the syrup. Remove from heat, stir in 1 cup of sugar. Cover with a napkin and put the lid on. Let stand for an hour before serving. Before transferring to a serving platter or individual serving dishes, stir to obtain fluffy appearance of semolina.

Sprinkle with cinnamon and garnish with powdered sugar. Serve at room temperature.
16-18 servings.

LADY'S NAVEL
Hanım Göbeği

SYRUP
1 cup (250 ml) water
2 cups (360 gr) sugar
1 tablespoon lemon
  juice

DOUGH
1¾ cup (437 ml) water
½ cup (100 gr) butter
1 teaspoon sugar
½ teaspoon salt
1¼ cup (125 gr) flour
4 eggs
1 tablespoon oil (for
  fingers)
oil for deep frying

Bring water to a boil, dissolve the sugar in the water. Cook for 5 minutes until a thick syrup is formed, add lemon juice. Set aside. Cool.

Pour water into a saucepan, add butter, sugar, salt and bring to a boil. Sift the flour and add it all at once, stirring constantly. Stir vigorously until the mixture forms a ball around the spoon and leaves the sides of the pan. Remove from the heat and cool. Add 1 egg at a time beating thoroughly after each addition. Chill the mixture for 30 minutes. Oil your fingers and form the dough into walnut-size balls. Flatten them slightly. Make a hole in the center. Deep fry in oil pre-heated to 300ºF (150ºC) until puffed up and golden brown. Transfer from the oil to the cold syrup with a perforated kitchen spoon, making sure that each lady's navel is drained for 10 minutes. Serve cold.

8 servings.

CHERRY BREAD
Vişneli Ekmek

1 ⅔ lbs (750 gr) pitted
  morello cherries
¾ cup (187.5 ml)
  water
1 lb (450 gr) sugar
1 loaf of day-old white
  bread, cut in thick
  slices, crusts removed
GARNISH
½ lb (225 gr) Turkish
  kaymak or whipped
  cream

Place cherries into a saucepan. Stir in the sugar. Set aside for half an hour. Stir in water and cook over medium heat for about 10 minutes until water becomes syrup. Set aside.

Toast slices of bread in the oven until crisp. Then put them on a platter, pour over the hot cherries and syrup. Cool.

Garnish with Turkish kaymak or whipped cream.

10 servings.

SEMOLINA CAKE
Revani

SYRUP	To make the syrup, heat water, add
6 cups (1½ liters) water	sugar and bring it to a boil. Add
3 cups (540 gr) sugar	lemon juice. Lower the heat and
1 tablespoon lemon	simmer for 10 minutes. Cool at room
juice	temperature. Set aside.
6 eggs	Place butter in a large mixing bowl
½ lb (225 gr) butter	and beat with a mixer for 1-2 minutes.
1 cup (180 gr) sugar	Stir in the sugar and then add the
1¼ cups (125 gr) flour	eggs 1 at a time. Beat in the flour and
1¼ cups (200 gr)	semolina gradually. Add the vanilla
semolina	and baking powder and stir until the
1 teaspoon vanilla	mixture is well blended.
2 teaspoons baking	Pour this mixture into a greased
powder	baking dish of 8 x 12 - inch (20 x 30 cm),
GARNISH	and bake in a pre-heated oven at
1 cup (100 gr)	350ºF (180ºC) for about 25-30 minutes
almonds, or	until golden brown.
pistachio nuts,	As soon as you take the semolina
grated	cake out of the oven, put a spatula in
½ cup (40 gr) coconut,	the sides of the baking pan and make
grated	sure the cake is not sticking. Cut into
½ lb (225 gr) whipped	squares of desired dimensions and
cream or Turkish	pour the cooled syrup gradually over
kaymak (optional)	the steaming hot cake. The cake will
(see page 84)	absorb most of the syrup. Serve with
	whipped cream or kaymak.

12 servings.

NIGHTINGALE'S NEST
Bülbül Yuvası

FILLING
2 cups (200 gr)
  walnuts, finely
  chopped
1 tablespoon sugar
¼ teaspoon ground
  cinnamon

PASTRY
12 frozen phyllo
  strudel leaves
1 cup (200 gr)
  unsalted butter,
  melted

SYRUP
1½ cups (270 gr)
  sugar
1¼ cups (312 ml)
  water
juice of ½ lemon

GARNISH
¼ cup (25 gr)
  pistachio nuts,
  ground or walnuts,
  ground

Make walnut filling by mixing all ingredients in a bowl. Set aside.

Place one phyllo leaf on a clean surface. Brush with butter. Sprinkle 1 tablespoon walnut filling evenly over the sheet. Place a thin 1 - inch (2.5 cm) rolling pin at the narrow end of the sheet and roll the pastry on the pin until the end. Push gently the rolled-up pastry on the pin from both ends towards the center to form wrinkles. Pull out the rolling pin. Form a spiral shape and place on a buttered baking tray. Bake in moderate oven about 30 minutes, until golden brown.

While nightingale nests are baking boil sugar and water, for 15 minutes. Add lemon juice 2 minutes before removing from heat.

Pour lukewarm syrup over hot nests, allow time to absorb syrup and cool. Transfer to a serving platter. Garnish with ground pistachio nuts or walnuts. Serve with whipped cream.
6 servings.

MINT AND LEMON DRINK
Nane Limon

peel of ½ lemon
2½ cups (625 ml) water
1 teaspoon dried mint
* or 4 fresh mint*
* leaves*

Peel lemon. Care should be taken not to cut through the pith so as to avoid a bitter taste.

Bring water to a boil. Add mint and lemon peel. Stir once and boil for 1 minute. Strain into teacups. Serve hot as a digestive or cure for upset stomachs. Drink with or without sugar. **2 servings.**

BEVERAGES
MINT AND LEMON DRINK
AYRAN
TURKISH COFFEE

YOGHURT DRINK
Ayran

$\frac{1}{2}$ cup (125 gr)
  yoghurt
$\frac{1}{2}$ cup (125 ml) cold
  water
salt to taste
2 fresh mint leaves
  (optional)

Place yoghurt into a bowl and stir until it becomes a creamy consistency, add water and salt and mix well. Or, place yoghurt, water and salt into a blender and blend at high speed for 1 minute. Pour into a long glass.

Garnish with mint leaves. Refrigerate before serving as a refreshing drink.

1 serving.

TURKISH TEA
Çay

6 cups (1$\frac{1}{2}$ liters) water
4 teaspoons tea leaves
1 teaspoon sugar
1 teaspoon water
4 lemon slices
  (optional)

Pour water into a kettle. Remove lid and place a smaller kettle on top to act as a double boiler. Place tea leaves and sugar into the small kettle and sprinkle with 1 teaspoon water. Cover with lid.

Bring water to a boil and pour $\frac{1}{3}$ of the boiling water over the tea leaves and sugar mixture. Cover. Replace it on top of the bigger kettle and let it brew for 6 minutes.

Strain brewed tea into teacups or small Turkish tea glasses, as much as desired, and dilute with boiling water according to taste. A lemon slice can be put in the cup if a lemony flavor is preferred. Drink with or without sugar.

Boiling water can be added to the smaller kettle to obtain more brewed tea.

4 servings.

TURKISH COFFEE
Türk Kahvesi

*1 heaped teaspoon
ground coffee*
*¼ teaspoon sugar (for
coffee with little
sugar)*
*½ teaspoon sugar (for
medium-sweet coffee)*
*1 teaspoon sugar (for
sweet coffee)*
*no sugar (for black
coffee)*
*¼ cup (62.5 ml) cold
water (or measure
water with demitasse
to be served)*

Turkish coffee can be obtained
anywhere as ground coffee.
Otherwise, coffee beans can be
roasted in a pan or in the oven
stirring occasionally until the
preferred darkness is obtained. Then
the beans are ground, if available, in a
Turkish "kahve değirmeni" (brass
coffee grinder) or in an ordinary
coffee grinder until it becomes
pulverized.

Ground coffee can be preserved in a
tightly-covered jar for a few weeks.

Place coffee and sugar into a small
cezve (pot with long handle,
preferably brass, copper or enamel),
add water and mix them together.
Cook on a very low heat stirring
occasionally until the froth on the
surface starts rising.

Pour a small amount of froth into a
demi-tasse. Return pot to the heat and
bring to a boil. Pour remaining coffee
into the demi-tasse until it reaches the
brim.

NOTE

If more than one demi-tasse is
preferred multiply above ingredients
by the number of the cups and pour a
little froth into each cup first. Make
sure not to drink the thick residue
remaining at the bottom of the coffee
cup.

1 serving.

INDEX

117